W9-BNL-421

Modern Southeast Asia Series

Stephen F. Maxner, General Editor

Also in the Series

DAVID &
LEE ROY

DAVID & LEE ROY

A Vietnam Story

David L. Nelson and Randolph B. Schiffer

Texas Tech University Press

This book is typeset in Stempel Schneidler. The paper used in this book meets
the minimum requirements of ANSI/NISO Z39.48-1992 (R1997). ∞

Designed by Kasey McBeath

Library of Congress Cataloging-in-Publication Data
Nelson, David L. (David Leon), 1944–
     David and Lee Roy : a Vietnam story / David L. Nelson and Randolph B.
Schiffer.
          p. cm. — (Modern Southeast Asia series)
     Includes index.
     Summary: "The story of David Nelson and Lee Roy Herron, friends from
Lubbock, Texas, during the Vietnam War. Describes Nelson's quest to uncover
the events leading to Lee Roy's 1969 death in service to the US Marine Corps,
providing closure and honoring the life of a fallen soldier"—Provided by publisher.
     ISBN 978-0-89672-694-9 (hardcover : alk. paper)
1. Nelson, David L. (David Leon), 1944– 2. Herron, Lee Roy, 1945–1969.
 3. Vietnam War, 1961-1975—Personal narratives, American. 4. Vietnam War,
1961–1975—Campaigns—Vietnam—Quang Tri (Province) 5. United States.
Marine Corps—Officers—Biography. 6. Lubbock (Tex.)—Biography. I. Schiffer,
Randolph B. II. Title.
     DS559.5.N45 2011
     959.704'345092—dc22
     [B]   2011015300

Printed in the United States of America
11 12 13 14 15 16 17 18 19 / 9 8 7 6 5 4 3 2 1

Texas Tech University Press
Box 41037 | Lubbock, Texas 79409-1037 USA
800.832.4042 | ttup@ttu.edu | www.ttupress.org

Naming no names, we dedicate this book to the women who waited for the Marines of the Vietnam War. These words are for them. For those who could not bear this terrible vigil, forgiveness. For those who lived to see the welcome day, gratitude. For those who keep till now the folded flag, acceptance of what was fated and could not be changed.

I had never been sure how Lee Roy was killed
    that day, back in 1969. Not really sure.
I had never thought much about what it meant
    to be a hero; what it was, or if it made any
    difference many years later.
I had always told myself that it didn't matter, what
    had happened. Lee Roy was dead, and I was
    alive, and life had to go on.
That was the way things were.
But that was wrong. I have come to realize now
    that I am grown old that it does matter what
    happened.
It matters to me.
My name is David Nelson.
Lee Roy was my friend.

Contents

Illustrations

Series Editor's Note

As editor of the Modern Southeast Asia Series, rarely have I come across a manuscript with so powerful a connection to the Vietnam Center and Archive, and its mission. There is also a strong connection to Texas Tech University and to West Texas, but *David and Lee Roy* is an American story—as rooted in any other U.S. town that sent friends to war as it is in Lubbock. It tells of two young men who grew up together before and during the Vietnam War, became the closest of friends, and followed the same life path to service in the United States Marine Corps. But their paths separated from there. David Nelson went to law school to serve as an attorney while Lee Roy Herron went to Vietnam to serve in combat. David survived the Vietnam War while Lee Roy was killed in action during Operation Dewey Canyon in A Shau Valley, Republic of Vietnam.

What is very special about this story is that it does not really end with the death of Lee Roy Herron on February 22, 1969. In some ways, that is something of a beginning. David Nelson's eventual "search for Lee Roy" brought him back to Lubbock and Texas Tech University. While here, he met Dr. Jim Reckner, founding director of the Vietnam Center and Archive. Together with Texas Tech Chancellor John Montford and other Vietnam Center supporters, David and Jim went to Vietnam. While traveling together they conceived of an idea to honor and memorialize Lee Roy and his service during the Vietnam War.

When they returned to Texas Tech, David approached his fellow classmates from Lubbock High School and together some of them decided to establish the Lee Roy Herron Endowed Scholarship at Texas Tech University to be administered by the Vietnam Center. The purpose for the scholarship was and is to provide opportunities for Texas Tech students to travel to Southeast Asia and learn firsthand about the peoples and cultures of that region of the world. From a desire to memorialize a friend, David Nelson and others created what has become one of the most profound learning and life experiences for the students selected to receive these scholarships. To date, the endowment contains $250,000 and has supported nearly fifty students who have engaged in the Vietnam Center Summer Study Abroad in Southeast Asia.

This book is also timely, as the United States is now engaged in a nationwide commemoration of the fiftieth anniversary of the Vietnam War. The U.S. Congress has passed legislation and established a federal program that will support commemoration activities at all levels in cities and towns around the country through 2025. As communities are seeking ways to remember and honor their Vietnam veterans, it is my hope that they will learn from the story of *David and Lee Roy* and will create similar educational programs that will help future generations remember the service and sacrifices of the Vietnam generation. For I disagree with authors who claim that one generation is greater than others. Instead, I believe that each generation faces its own unique set of challenges and that each deserves to be thanked and recognized for doing its best in taking on and overcoming them.

More widespread recognition for our nation's Vietnam veterans and the Vietnam generation is long overdue.

David and Lee Roy is written in the style of a memoir, and the result is a personal and emotional story. The authors recall conversations and convey them in a way that transports the reader back in time. Readers must keep in mind, though, that while some of these conversations took place in the presence of the authors, others did not. To help maintain the writing style, the authors interviewed others about their conversations with Lee Roy and took some literary license in recreating dialogue they believe to have taken place.

Acknowledgments

The two of us primarily involved in the writing of *David and Lee Roy* worked at it over a period of thirteen years, and along this way there were several junctures wherein key assistance from others probably saved us from failure.

First, we recognize Jeff Whitley, who in some ways had the originating ideas for the project, and who worked alongside us throughout—interviewing persons with stories to tell, lending his technological expertise to our imaging work, and encouraging us at every juncture.

Jane Herron Graham and Lorea Herron, Lee Roy's sister and mother, respectively, blessed this work, and encouraged us. There were many painful moments of remembrance for them as the writing proceeded, from which it is difficult to see benefit for them beyond the good that comes from leaving testament to history. Had they not agreed to the book, we could not have written it.

James Reckner, director of the Vietnam Center at Texas Tech University until his retirement in 2009, consistently reminded us of what we had believed at the beginning—that there would be value in the telling of this story. He helped with the reading of early drafts of the work, and he assisted us with several important aspects of the March 3, 2001, ceremony in honor of Lee Roy Herron.

From the class of 1963 of Lubbock High School, Lee Roy's class, we wish to publicly recognize Maureen Malley Peltier, Marcie Cates Johnston Beasley, Bill Cox, Jr., and Jimmy Davis. All four worked with us in the collecting of background information for the book, and in the preparation of the March 3, 2001, ceremony. With sadness, we recognize Marcie's death from cancer in 2007.

Last, we recognize Norman Flanagan, who crafted the bronze relief of Lee Roy to be unveiled at the 2001 ceremony, and to rest into the future in the Vietnam Center at Texas Tech University. Sadly, Norman, too, has now passed from this world.

Authors' Note

We didn't think it would be that hard, the writing of *David and Lee Roy*. We would review the papers that David Nelson had collected over the years. We would interview David's and Lee Roy's family and friends in West Texas. We would interview survivors of Alpha Company, First Battalion, Ninth Marines, Lee Roy's final Marine unit. Then we would write those facts down, and that would be it. Indeed, we did it just that way. We collected all those facts and wrote down a certain kind of story about David Nelson and Lee Roy Herron, two young men who grew up in West Texas in the 1950s and 1960s.

Yet something was missing. The facts were there, but not the most important things: the experience of it all in the 1960s; the relationships reaching across time and beyond death; the terrible dark drama of the Vietnam War.

And so, we redrew the characters in certain ways. We tried to make them come alive by reconstructing their words and actions at key junctures and during critical events. Through some necessary creative license we tried to have the characters of the book tell the story to the reader, as opposed to our telling it. This was especially interesting for us, because one of us *is* David Nelson, and one of us *did* go where Lee Roy went.

No character in the book is completely fictitious. But we have changed the names of some of the minor figures, and we have wrapped up some of them into composites who could better show the drama of the moments.

All major facts and dates are correct historically, as best we could determine them.

The saddest thing for us is that we could not show the story to Lee Roy. We could not ask him if we had got it right, the way he would have wanted it. But sometimes we felt him with us in the writing, and so we hope he will not take offense if we sign his name here, with ours.

Lee Roy Herron
David L. Nelson
Randolph B. Schiffer

Preface

Always there have been the wars. And the wars have come to the young men, and the young men have made their choices. In their turn, the wars have chosen. The wars have said that some young men shall live and some shall die. Only the years can understand these things. The stories are there, but it takes the years to understand them. We have waited to write these stories until we ourselves are grown old. Even so, we are not sure we have understood.

In *David and Lee Roy* we tell the story of two young men who grew up together in West Texas in the 1960s. Both attended Texas Tech University. Both became Marine Corps officers after that. But the choices came, and one went to Vietnam and one did not. One died and one lived.

David and Lee Roy is a story of heroism, but it is difficult to say just what heroism is. There is heroism in death and there is heroism in life. *David and Lee Roy* has stories about both.

We think of *David and Lee Roy* as a story about all young men in the 1960s in America, not just about two. The war in Vietnam came, and it came for all of us, and it brought with it choices. No one wanted it. One could fight. One could flee. One could try for something in between. But the choices came, and the young men made them.

Later, much later, regrets came for all. Some lived to feel bad about what they had done, some about what they had not done. *David and Lee Roy* tells the story of regret, loss, and longing never made right. We, the authors, were there, too, and we have felt these longings awaken, and at times it has been painful for us in the writing. Yet time has said finally of each choice that it was as it had to be, that it could not be changed, and acceptance has come finally to us all. We believe that this acceptance can be seen in this book as well.

It has not been easy for us to write *David and Lee Roy*, since we have been on both sides, past and the present. We were there and we are here, and at times it has been difficult to know the truth. Major facts, events, and dates are represented as accurately as we have known them, but we have altered some details, some contexts, and some emphases to better capture the measure of the story. For example, there were many battlefield heroes in the A Shau Valley the day Lee Roy was killed, but we have chosen to keep our focus upon Lee's actions that day, as best we know them. Other scenarios, while describing fictional events and conversations, could very well have taken place. The really important parts of the book relate true incidents that we knew of personally or were told of by others.

We have written *David and Lee Roy* primarily for ourselves, but we hope that others, too, will find answers, even as we have done. Answers for themselves, for those close to them, and for those they remember.

DAVID & LEE ROY

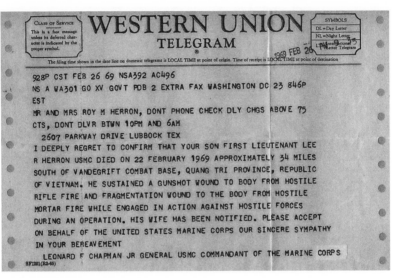

WESTERN UNION
TELEGRAM

The filing time shown in the date line on domestic telegrams is LOCAL TIME at point of origin. Time of receipt is LOCAL TIME at point of destination

1969 FEB 26

928P CST FEB 26 69 NSA392 AC496

NS A WA301 GO XV GOVT PDB 2 EXTRA FAX WASHINGTON DC 23 846P
EST

MR AND MRS ROY M HERRON, DONT PHONE CHECK DLY CHGS ABOVE 75
CTS, DONT DLVR BTWN 10PM AND 6AM
  2607 PARKWAY DRIVE LUBBOCK TEX
I DEEPLY REGRET TO CONFIRM THAT YOUR SON FIRST LIEUTENANT LEE
R HERRON USMC DIED ON 22 FEBRUARY 1969 APPROXIMATELY 34 MILES
SOUTH OF VANDEGRIFT COMBAT BASE, QUANG TRI PROVINCE, REPUBLIC
OF VIETNAM. HE SUSTAINED A GUNSHOT WOUND TO BODY FROM HOSTILE
RIFLE FIRE AND FRAGMENTATION WOUND TO THE BODY FROM HOSTILE
MORTAR FIRE WHILE ENGAGED IN ACTION AGAINST HOSTILE FORCES
DURING AN OPERATION. HIS WIFE HAS BEEN NOTIFIED. PLEASE ACCEPT
ON BEHALF OF THE UNITED STATES MARINE CORPS OUR SINCERE SYMPATHY
IN YOUR BEREAVEMENT
  LEONARD F CHAPMAN JR GENERAL USMC COMMANDANT OF THE MARINE CORPS

SF1201(R2-65)

Telegram received by Lee Roy Herron's parents. Courtesy of the Herron family.

[1]
This Was What He Wanted

March 5, 1969

Lubbock, Texas

I wasn't there that day, when Lee Roy came home. I suppose some people thought I should have been, since Lee Roy and I were so close growing up. No one ever said that, but some of them were thinking it, I'm sure. But they didn't understand. I was in law school at that time, at Southern Methodist University School of Law, in Dallas. They didn't understand what that was like, second year in a law school. It was tough. There were courses on tax law, community property, torts, and many other topics. There were readings every day, and you couldn't fall behind. You couldn't just take off for something, come back, and think that you'd catch right up. No. I just couldn't take the time off, when Lee Roy came home.

The winds blow cold in Lubbock in March. They blow dust from the west in the late afternoon, and the dust turns the skies dark brown.

The Continental Airlines plane came in from the east, bucking and heaving against the wind. The aircraft made slow progress toward the crisscrossing asphalt runways of the Lubbock airport, set amidst cotton fields. The pilot brought the plane down close to the cotton, the wind and the dust bucked the aged propeller blades, the wings flapped up and down, and the engines whined and groaned. It was as if even the wind was saying no to the task that lay ahead.

Inside the terminal, standing alone against tinted glass, a diminutive woman watched the plane as it approached. She wore a brown coat, buttoned close against her chest, its cuffs showing years of use. The plane looked like a toy, she thought. Across the darkened distance of the airfield, it looked small and silvery, with some orange along its side. In her mind's eye she could see the toy airplanes her little son had held at Christmas. He had sat cross-legged under the Christmas tree and whooshed the toy airplanes in his hands to and fro between its branches. She remembered how her boy had done that, and she was silent.

The plane landed, coming down hard on the cold asphalt, with two spurts of rubber burn trailing behind. The woman in the brown coat waited. From the window she watched the plane taxi from across the distant runway to the terminal building. The plane was coming to her, and she was waiting for it.

The Lubbock airport terminal was an elongated, sixties-style rectangular structure that had pastel plastic panels alternating with its windows. The woman in the brown coat watched with others as the plane arrived outside those windows, all busy with its propellers turning, its fuselage silver, with bright-orange suns on both sides. The pilots cut the engines. The ground crew tacked blocks beneath the wheels and fixed wire lines to stanchions in the asphalt, and the lines pulled tight against the wind.

The propellers slowed gradually, then stopped. The pilots removed their headsets, looking down at the controls first, and then glancing up through the windshield of the plane, looking into the terminal briefly. The waiting woman could see them looking up toward where she stood.

A few passengers came out the door of the airplane, holding their coats around them as they climbed down the swaying metal stairs. They held aluminum railings to steady themselves, and when they reached the tarmac they hurried to the entrance doors of the terminal and disappeared inside. There were few such passengers in March in West Texas. People didn't come there that time of year in those days, unless they had some job to do, or unless they were coming home.

Inside there were more stairs, coming up to the window level of the terminal. The sounds of footsteps muttered on the wooden stairs, and when the passengers were up to the corridor of the windows, there were family and friends waiting for them. There were greetings and smiles, and then they walked away in twos and fours until none were left. The plain woman in the plain coat was still waiting.

After a time, after the others had come and gone, five more passengers came from the plane, blinking into the wind. Walking slowly, single file, they made their way down the rolling stairs, all dressed in blues and reds that stood out against the brown of the dust-blown day. Inside, the waiting woman watched them.

They were four enlisted marines and one officer, each wearing the dress-blue uniform of the Marine Corps in winter, close-buttoned, with black shoes polished to gleaming, and, above their left breast pockets, rows of ribbons of the war.

The marines moved to the tail of the aircraft, where ground crew perched upon the open ledge of the cargo compartment. When it was time, the latter slid off a green steel casket, sent it down a steel ramp, and the waiting marines took hold of it, one enlisted man on each corner. The lieutenant stood to the side. Carrying the casket quickly to a waiting pickup, a gray Ford with the black lettering of the Naval Reserve on its doors, the marines slid it into the truck bed. The lieutenant walked behind and glanced up quickly at the watching windows of the terminal, wondering who was there.

Holding their caps against the late-winter winds, the marines eased themselves into a second vehicle waiting there, a sedan the same gray and black as the truck, and the small motorcade drove off, around the corner of the terminal building, and toward the open roads of the West Texas plains beyond.

The small woman in the brown coat had left her window by the time the pickup had rounded the corner.

The Resthaven Cemetery in Lubbock spreads out against the western edges of the city, where the pioneer founders laid it in the early years of the twentieth century. They had placed the cemetery outside the young city, across a flat space of pinion pine trees that no one owned, nor was much interested in. In the beginning they had described the cemetery as "rolling" and "peaceful," but since there was really nothing rolling about the place, over time they had come to call it merely peaceful. There had been nothing but the land in the beginning, but over time some mortuary buildings had accumulated in the southwest corner of the place, and here the Naval Reserve pickup truck stopped, with the sedan behind. The marines carried the coffin inside a small anteroom whose doors protruded into the few parking spots there, and they set it upon the steel rollers of a rectangular resting mount. Then they waited there for the plain Texas woman in the plain coat. And soon she came.

She entered the Resthaven Funeral Home, with its viewing

rooms, embalming rooms, and crematorium tucked discreetly along the northwest corner of the building. It was a place of death, despite the softness of the carpets and the crafted paintings on the walls. It was a place of death, and Lee Roy had come home to it.

"I'm Andy Vaart, Mrs. Herron," said the lieutenant as the woman entered the concrete room.

"Thank you for coming, Andy," she said. The officer stood between her and the casket. The four enlisted men stood against the wall, at parade rest with their hands clasped behind them, their black shoes spread at shoulder width.

She looked past the lieutenant to the green casket in the center of the room. She moved toward it, and she gently placed her left hand on its side.

"Lee Roy spoke of you, Andy," she said to the officer.

"Open it, please," she said.

The room was silent. The marines stood still, and time slowed to ticking moments in the clock of life and death.

"You don't have to open it, Mrs. Herron," said the lieutenant, but he said it demurely, respectfully, as if he knew the words were futile and that soon he would have to open the casket.

"I want to see him," she said.

"The Marine Corps has certified that it's him, Mrs. Herron," said the lieutenant, still protesting softly against what he and his men would soon do and did not want to do.

"Open it," she said. She stepped back from the steel box, taking her hand off it, but she kept her eyes on it, and she looked at nothing else.

The officer nodded to the marines along the wall. Two lance corporals stepped forward, socket wrenches in their hands, and they loosened the octagonal bolts along the edges of the casket and pulled them from their holes. When this was done, they hesitated and looked back to Lieutenant Vaart. He nodded. The two corporals came to help. They lifted up the lid of the coffin from the grooves in which it had rested. They slid the lid off at an angle to the floor, and they stepped back.

The diminutive woman in the simple cloth coat stepped forward and looked over the edge of the coffin. She looked into it, and she was close to it.

She peered into it for a time, and there was stillness in the room. She was still looking in when she spoke.

"That is him," she said. She was still looking in, and she spoke again. "He is more suntanned than when he left," she said. She was still looking at him, but the others looked away.

"This was what he wanted," she said. And then she stepped back from the coffin, turned away from it, and left the room.

The enlisted men stepped forward again. They slid the lid back over the top of the casket. They returned the octagonal bolts to their places, and they tightened them. And then they stood back against the concrete walls and clasped their hands behind their backs. The officer stepped forward and placed a folded flag across the coffin, and then he opened it carefully, the red and white and blue covering the green steel. He turned to look at the woman, but she had gone.

"Is that all there is to it, Lieutenant?" asked one of the corporals.

"I guess so," said Lieutenant Vaart. "I guess that's all there is to it."

The marines turned, and walked away, and one of the grounds crew looked in from the viewing room door and turned out the lights.

In a photo that appeared in a March 1969 issue of the *Lubbock Avalanche-Journal* newspaper, Lee Roy Herron's widow Danelle reads his last letters, including one to be delivered in case of his death. Courtesy of the *Lubbock Avalanche-Journal*.

[2]
There Was One Stout Lieutenant from West Texas

August 2, 1997

Houston, Texas

Houston Endowment

I didn't think about Lee Roy much after his death. I didn't see any point to it. Life has to go on. That's what I told myself, and I believe I was right. You can't dwell in the past. I was married. I had to finish law school, had to serve my time as a judge advocate general (JAG) officer in the Marines, had to raise the children, had to make the career go. There were a lot of "have tos" during those years. I'm not complaining. I'm just saying how it was. Lee Roy would have understood, I told myself. Lee Roy never had to face these things. Occasionally, when there was so much to do and I just didn't know if I could do it all, I did think of Lee Roy, and I envied him briefly. That was strange, I know, feeling envy for someone like Lee Roy, who had been killed. You can't let thoughts like that come into your mind, of course, so when such thoughts came I would tell myself that I had no time to think about Lee Roy. That worked pretty well until August 2, 1997.

That day, a Thursday, Harriet, my administrative assistant at Houston Endowment, placed a clipping from the newspaper on my desk:

> Colonel Wesley Fox, USMC (ret) will be pleased to sign copies of his book, *Marine Rifleman*, at the Borders bookstore in the Standard Oil Building, first floor, at six PM today.

Black words, with black lines around them.

My office was in the corner of the twenty-second floor of the Jones Building in Houston.

I looked down at the blinking lights on the telephone console in the center of a large desk, irritable lights, each one a caller with a complaint or a request. I had looked at them all day, I remember very clearly, and suddenly I didn't care about those lights. I didn't care what those people wanted or what their complaints were.

I swiveled my chair around. I turned my back to the blinking lights of the telephone console, and I looked out the floor-length glass windows of the office, gazing west. It was summer in Houston, and the sun was still thirty degrees above the horizon, shining deep indigoes through the darkened glass. There was a great southern city down below me, but I was looking far beyond it—to the west, where Lubbock was.

"Aren't you going to answer the calls, Mr. Nelson?"

I looked back around. It was Harriet. She was standing there in the doorway between my office and her paneled office just outside. I swiveled my chair again and sat facing her.

Harriet was a handsome woman, I thought, looking at her that day. Trim, wire-rimmed spectacles, demure gray suit. You could look at her and see her in different ways, I noticed that day. You could see her as an old woman, a career administrator, dry and thin and weak. But you could also look at her and see an attractive woman, fit, sensitive, totally in control of herself. I hadn't noticed that until that day. I realized then that you could look at most things two ways. I also realized that I didn't know Harriet. She had been with me for all those years at Houston Endowment, and I didn't really know who she was.

But Harriet had come to know me in a deep and personal way. I realized it as if for the first time that day, at that moment when the newspaper clipping appeared on my desk. Did Harriet know that I had been in the Marines myself those many years ago? Had I made it that obvious? I hadn't been aware of it. But if I hadn't been aware of that, what else about myself had Harriet seen, that I had not? What else was there for her to see? There was something wrong here, I could tell. This wasn't how I had always seen myself.

There was a very slight smile along the edges of Harriet's eyes. She was amused at my letting the blinking lights go. The most conscientious of administrative assistants was amused that I was flaking off the business of the endowment. And then there was the newspaper clipping. Yes. Harriet had seen something in me, something that was coming or changing, and she had seen it before I had.

"Shall I tell the callers that you have left for the day, Mr. Nelson?" Harriet smiled. There was a glint of light from the western sun reflecting from her glasses.

I didn't know what to say. I tend to the quiet side, especially at times when things are moving, and that quietness has been a wise confidant for me over the years. I thought I would just wait, to hear what Harriet would say next.

"I saw that clipping in the newspaper, and I thought it might be good for you to go, Mr. Nelson," she said. "I thought perhaps you had known this Colonel Fox in your youth."

She did know about me. She knew about my being in the Marines in the 1960s. Had I been indiscreet? Had I said things about myself that I shouldn't have said? How could Harriet have known these things? I wondered, and I was suddenly unsure.

"Anyway," said Harriet, and now she walked into my office, and she was pulling down the blinds and straightening the pillows on the chairs, as she did each night after I left. She was signaling to me that I should go, should leave the office now though this early departure hadn't been planned. "Anyway," she said again, "I thought it was time for you to attend this book signing."

Harriet didn't even look at me. She continued her tidying, and it was settled.

"All right, Harriet," I said. I couldn't help but smile at her. Something was coming inside me, and she had seen it before I had.

"And Harriet," I said, "could I ask you to call Mrs. Nelson, and tell her that I've got to attend a conference at the Standard Oil Building for dinner tonight, and I'll be home later?"

"I already did," said Harriet. And she left the room, returning to her desk, and the oaken door closed shut behind her.

After Harriet had closed the door, I didn't leave right away. There was a back exit from my office, and back elevators in the building, so no one was going to notice when I left. But I didn't go right away. It was very unusual for me to leave the office during regular hours like that. My position was an important one, and when you're in a position like that you can't just walk out of the office without it being in the printed daily schedule. Not if you were vice president and grant director at Houston Endowment. No. I tried to analyze it, what was happening; to break things apart into little bits so they could be added in columns— accounted and understood. That's how I had always tried to decide things. You have to add up the positives and the negatives, and that will give you the answer. But not that day. What was happening wouldn't go into the columns that day.

I looked at the clipping again. It was from that day's *Houston Chronicle*, the "Events in Houston" page. "Colonel Wesley Fox, USMC (ret)."

Col. Wesley Fox. Of course, it was true. I had known Colonel Fox. Long ago, when I had been at The Basic School for Marine Corps officers at Quantico, Virginia, sometimes known as TBS. He had been an instructor there. He had returned from his Vietnam tour a year before, and he had a Medal of Honor. A sky-blue ribbon with five white stars. Of course I remembered him. But that had been long ago. I told myself that I couldn't even remember those days. But I was leaving the office, and going to this book signing. Harriet had seen that I should go, and I was going.

I placed the clipping in the side pocket of my briefcase, and turned out the lamp on the desk to save electricity, even though it had one of the new energy-efficient bulbs. I walked out, using the corner door, which led to elevators through the back hallway, and then to a small lobby at the side of the building, and then outside to busy sidewalks and the bright sun of Texas. Two blocks away was the Borders bookstore in the Standard Oil Building. I left the rotating exit doors and turned toward it.

In the bookstore the coolness of the air conditioning was refreshing, as was the quiet of the readers after the rush-hour business and pushiness of the Houston sidewalks outside. I don't like pushy and aggressive people. Of course, I had come to this bookstore before, but always when I had to buy something. Sometimes I had come to buy books for trips, or as gifts, things like that. I had never come in the store just to look around, however. And I had never paid much attention to the kind of people who had time to come there for an author signing. But there I was that day, doing just that.

I blinked my eyes after leaving the bright sunlight, and tried to find some orientation in the cool relative darkness of the store.

There were rows and shelves of books in the store, all branching at right angles to the center aisle. At the far end of the aisle was a squat desk with an information sign in front of it, and a very thin young woman sitting behind it. She was so thin that it looked as if she had no figure at all. Just two thin arms, a smock-like shirt that extended below her knees and doubled as a dress, and her bespectacled eyes. Those two eyes grown large in the glass of the lenses told who she was. I figured if anybody knew what was what in the bookstore it would be her.

I went over to the desk to ask her. It was a little awkward for me. She didn't look up right away, which made it worse, me standing there like that. I had a sudden fear that someone I knew might see me there, recognize me, and even ask me what I was doing. I secretly scanned the customers, to see if any board members of Houston Endowment might be sidling their way between the rows of books. But there were none.

The information lady was reading. She was reading a children's book, *Where the Wild Things Are*, and on its cover were all kinds of furry beasts. It probably sounds strange, but I had a terrible, sudden fear that I might end up like that—reading children's books in the middle of the day.

"Excuse me," I said. I had to interrupt the monsters in the children's book. She looked up at me. She really was far too thin, I thought. Her face was so angular, as if carved sharply from some block of pain and suffering that had led her to the silence of the Borders store, where she could read children's books and not be disturbed. She looked up at me as if I were someone who had come to bother her. She continued to hold the book of furry monsters in her hands.

"Where is the reading?" I asked.

The information lady furrowed her thin brow, as if she had not understood the question. Then she turned her head, and looked behind her, up the few steps to the second-level area of the store. It was the children's section. My worst fears were coming true. And there, in the midst of rows and tables of picture books and teenage romance stories, was a modest crowd of people, sitting in neat rows of metal folding chairs. It seemed too late to turn back, especially with the anorexic information lady staring at me.

I went up the steps. The young woman went back to her book of furry creatures.

In the children's area, the reading had already begun. I came into the back row, and eased myself slowly into one of the chairs so it wouldn't creak.

In front, silhouetted against colorful displays of books with big and simple letters or large pictures of loyal dogs on the cover, set low on shelves for little hands to grasp them, and titles like *Jane and the Four Bar Ranch* and *The Crack of the Bat*, Col. Wesley Fox sat reading to the audience. On his table were three stacks of the book he had written, *Marine Rifleman*. The books looked new and crisp. They were for sale, I figured.

He didn't look like the Colonel Fox I had known at Quantico, now almost thirty years before. He looked old. His hair was white. There was a fleshiness about his face—the leanness and hardness that had been there when he had stood hyping us up to shoot and stab and burn make-believe enemies, that sharpness was gone. He was reading in a monotone from his own book there in the children's section of Borders, staring down at the pages through spectacles that slipped low on his nose continuously, which he would then push back up.

Colonel Fox was not a natural-born reader, I thought, as I sat and listened to him. He read with a somewhat stilted and awkward voice, as if some of the words and phrases had not hung together on their own for long, but had to be tied up and read just so or they might wander away from each other. He alternately peered down at the book and then looked up at the audience through the upper half of the bifocals that he wore.

Colonel Fox must be at least as uncomfortable as I am here, I thought, reading aloud in the children's section of a bookstore, with pictures of cats and dogs all about. It just wasn't like The Basic School at all.

I thought about leaving. I thought I might stand up, hunched over, and look urgently taken by some forgotten task or appointment. I could walk down the three steps and past the anorexic information girl, and no one would notice. I didn't think Colonel Fox had seen me. I told myself there had been a mistake.

But then I began to hear some of the words he was reading.

"And First Platoon came under intense fire from the hillside above them, and they were pinned down, and could not move either forward or backward." Colonel Fox peered up over his glasses. He looked at the audience, and now he spoke right to them, and I felt again the echoes of the leadership power that had been in him at The Basic School, and that had brought him the Medal of Honor.

"I was moving with the center of the column when the ambush hit from the hillside above us to the right. We were spread out and I had trouble getting my platoon commanders together to coordinate the return fires," he said.

Yes, I thought. I can imagine how it had been.

"We had men down, I could tell from the radio traffic, but it was all mixed up, confused. It was a bad situation."

I listened. I looked about at the others in the audience, and I wondered if they understood what this man was telling them, if they really had any idea of what it had been like. The others in the small audience were mostly women. They all seemed to be wearing glasses. None were young, and none looked old. There were a few scattered gray-haired men, mostly grown paunchy with the years. I wondered if some of these were the sort of middle-class, unreconstructed Vietnam veteran types whose lives were stuck on pause, continually reliving the only time in their lives when they had been part of something bigger than themselves. I had little respect for those men. I considered them the type who would tell their exaggerated war stories to anyone who would listen—the type who would ride wheelchairs down sunny streets in Memorial Day parades, when maybe they didn't even really need to be in the wheelchairs. I had never wanted to be like that. Of course, I had not exactly gone to Vietnam. But that had not been my fault. The Marine Corps had sent me where they had needed me most, and that was to law school and then Okinawa. The war in Vietnam had been almost over by the time I got there. It wasn't my fault.

Colonel Fox continued his reading.

"I coordinated the supporting fires, both air and artillery, and I reinforced Second Platoon with the reserve elements from Head-quarters group. Alpha Company brought increasing pressure to bear upon the entrenched enemy upon the rocky hillside." It was hard to follow, I thought. He had been a more dynamic speaker at TBS, I thought, where he never read from his notes.

As Colonel Fox read, I thought of other things in my life, things that had marked the course of it. I thought of my oldest daughter,

Amy. Amy had made a mistake, I thought, in marrying while she was in law school. She had married a guy she had met as an undergraduate, and it was not working out. I had foreseen that it would not work out, but Amy had not listened to me. And now they were divorcing. Colonel Fox was reading about the 9th Marines in Quang Tri Province, and I was thinking about our daughter Amy. It made no sense to me.

And then I heard something big. It wasn't that I actually consciously heard it, but I felt that something had been said that was different from the rest, important, important to me. Something Colonel Fox had just said. But what? And then it came again.

"And one stout young man from West Texas made the difference that day," Colonel Fox was saying, going over it again with some of the intensity in his voice that had been there long ago, and he had to pause. I wondered if a tear had come to his eye, but I could not see for sure. He was looking at the audience now. He was telling them something.

"Lee Herron, from Texas Tech University," he said. I thought, yes, there was a shining in his eyes, behind the lenses, tears from that day almost thirty years before.

"And when I got the word back that Lee was down," he continued—he was having trouble with the words, but he kept on—"and I got the word that Lee was down, and he had been hit hard. But the enemy fire had dropped, too, and I knew that Lee had done something up there on the hillside. I knew we were going to make it now."

Colonel Fox picked up the book, and he read on until the time of his reading was up. I listened. There was no more daydreaming for me now. I stared at the short man in the front and I could not get out of my mind what he had said.

When Colonel Fox's reading was over, everyone in the audience stood up. I stood up with them, although I felt somewhat mechanical, a bit like a robot. There was polite applause, and I too clapped. Most of those in the small audience left. I walked up to the front of the reading area.

A few of the bespectacled women and one of the middle-aged men were standing across the table from Colonel Fox. He was autographing his books for them, and he seemed more at ease bending over, making his marks inside the flyleaves of the books using a black felt-tip pen. Hanging out from his suit jacket as he bent forward to write was the sky-blue ribbon of the Medal of Honor, with its bronze, white-starred centerpiece swinging to and fro above the covers of the books.

I waited in the informal line in front of the table, to be the last. Colonel Fox looked up at me.

"Wesley Fox," he said, reaching out his hand to me, firm and strong as his words. I took his hand, but hesitantly.

"Would you like to buy one?" asked the colonel, pointing down at copies of *Marine Rifleman*.

"Yes," I said, but faintly. I wasn't sure what to say.

"Did you say yes?" asked the colonel.

"Yes," I said.

"Do you remember me, Colonel Fox?" I asked.

He looked up from his seat, studying my face, his eyes searching for a memory.

"No," he said. "Have we met before?"

"I was at The Basic School in 1971. TBS class 4-71. You were still an instructor there."

"What is your name?" asked Colonel Fox.

"David Nelson," I said.

"Semper Fi," he said.

I reached inside my jacket pocket and pulled out my wallet to pay for the book. Colonel Fox was writing his name on a flyleaf.

"Would you please write in it 'To David and Lee Roy'?" I asked. Without standing up, Colonel Fox looked up intently again.

"What?" he asked.

I felt suddenly ashamed. I can't tell you why. I can't tell you where it came from.

"Lee Roy and I were—" I spoke quickly, and then I paused. "I knew him," I said.

"You knew Lee Herron?" asked Colonel Fox, still bent partly over the table, not finished with the autographing, holding the pen poised in the air.

"No, no," I said quickly. "I mean—I went to college with him."

It was all so shameful. What I had just said had sounded terrible.

"I knew him some," I said. I was trying to close this off. I wanted to get the book and go. I was sorry I had requested that inscription. I told myself that I hadn't really known Lee Roy that well.

"How did you know Lee?" asked Colonel Fox. He still looked up at me, with his pen poised halfway to the flyleaf.

I couldn't think of what to say.

"He was my best friend," I said. And there it was. The words had taken their own way out.

Colonel Fox was still poised with the pen in his hand. "All right," he said, turning back down to the work at hand with the pen. "To David and Lee Roy," he said firmly as he wrote, and then it was done, and he closed the book and handed it to me.

"How much?" I asked.

"This one is a gift," said the colonel.

I reached out and took the book, and as I touched it I felt that the colonel and I had both crossed over a line in time, that from the words in the book we had felt the terrible power of that day in 1969 when Lee Roy and so many others had killed and been killed. We paused there, in the children's section of the Border's bookstore in Houston in 1997, and we felt the crossing of that line.

"I'm done with this now," said the colonel, and he waved his hand across the piles of *Marine Rifleman* on the table. "Have a coffee with me," he said, and he looked toward the Borders deli in the far corner of the store. He stood up.

Colonel Fox stood erect in a tan linen suit, almost khaki, I thought, almost as if he had gone to Brooks Brothers down the street to get some clothes that would make him look like an author, but it hadn't worked and he had come out still wearing khakis. My fantasy was that he was trying to move away from the person he had been that day in 1969—his hair was white now—and his publisher had told him to go to Brooks Brothers to get a new suit, but it had failed. He was still back there in the lines of those memories; time had not moved for him, nor would it ever.

"Fine," I said.

We walked past several shelves and aisles to the deli, where small, overpriced cups of espresso could be purchased, and where severely bookish people sat around small glass tables reading.

We took the dainty porcelain cups from the woman behind the counter and moved off to the side, away from the others who were there.

It seemed silly to me to be sipping espresso and chewing the little pieces of lemon that came with each cup, but Colonel Fox did not seem to mind.

"Tell me about Lee Herron," said the colonel. He said it as if he really wanted to know. I had the feeling that this man was not curious about many people. But he wanted to know about Lee Roy. He spoke again.

"I never really got to know him before—"

The colonel paused and the wrinkles in his face deepened with the pain of many memories, memories that I could see had never fit into the words of his book, pain never captured in a citation or a streamer on a flag. "Before that day."

"Tell me about Lee," he said.

I looked at Colonel Fox there in the Borders bookstore deli, and I felt the pain too. I was looking at Colonel Fox, but I was seeing Lee Roy. I was seeing Lee Roy now for the first time in many years.

[3]
1959
The Sun Shone Brightly

Lubbock, Texas

Both my grandfathers were cotton farmers on the Southern Plains, around the beginning of the twentieth century. They worked near a town called Becton, Texas, which was just off a Burlington Northern railroad stop twenty-four miles northeast of Lubbock, in a part of the country that was not yet really civilized. It is still dry and hard and flat—baked by the sun in the summer until cracks appear across the ground so large that small animals might fall in them and disappear. In the winter the land is lashed by mountain winds from the west and northwest. Many people think that the last place held out by Indians was in Idaho or Montana, but I think one of the last places was the staked plains of West Texas where the last free band of Comanches did not surrender until 1875. Some say they call the sports teams at Texas Tech the Red Raiders in memory of those people.

The town where my grandparents lived and worked has dwindled like so many others in the Southern Plains. In the 1970s a Baptist church closed in Becton. Elsewhere a church closing might not be a major problem, but in West Texas it pretty much means a town is dying when the Baptist church closes.

Our families never made much money at cotton farming. Pretty much nobody did. Preston Smith, who ran one of the movie theaters in Lubbock in the thirties and later became governor, used to say that the Kennedys missed the Great Depression because they were too rich to notice it and the Smiths in Lubbock missed the Depression because they were too poor to notice it.

My father, Edmund Nelson, was born and lived as a child north of Idalou and Lorenzo, then flat trail intersections in the cotton dust and nothing more. However, he was able to attend the Estacado school outside Lubbock for a few years when he was little, and I think that got it started—got a sense of opportunity and progress into him, even though really it would take the next generation, when I came, to fully instill that sense. He was able to attend the Lorenzo high school for a couple of years, only because he could walk to it. The school closed down in the fall when it was time to harvest the cotton, and other times of the year he couldn't go every day since the family did not have a car and it cost money to ride the bus. But going to high school had been something for my father. It was a start.

Education is the key, the key to success in America. In a way, you could say that it was education that decided that Lee Roy would die and I would live, a number of years later in the sixties. But I'm getting ahead of the story.

My father moved to Lubbock after high school, and he got a job as a salesman with the Ben E. Keith Company. He made enough so that my folks could live in a small house on Uvalde Avenue. This house had only four rooms: a bedroom, a bathroom, a kitchen, and a living room. A few years later a second bedroom was added after my older brother James and I came along. In 1959 we moved to 4406 West Fifteenth Street, in what would later become known as the Rush neighborhood in

Lubbock, after the name of the elementary school there. My parents built the cheapest house on the block in that neighborhood, and I remember hearing them argue about money late into the night. They disagreed about whether they could keep the house, and whether they should sell it and move to a poorer neighborhood. I hated to hear those arguments, sitting quietly in my pajamas on the floor, half in and half out of my bedroom down the hall. I never wanted it to be like that for my family. Imagining the future, I never wanted to argue in the night with my wife over whether we would have to sell our house.

Because we lived in the Rush neighborhood, I attended R. W. Matthews Junior High School in Lubbock, Texas. It was there that I met Lee Roy Herron. I remember it well.

Tuesday, September 22, 1959
R. W. Matthews Junior High School
Lubbock, Texas
Ninth-Grade Football Practice Field

"Why did you hit me so hard, Lee Roy?"

Lee Roy stood over me like the great Cyclops of Rhodes, straddling my chest. I lay in the middle of the dusty, sun-baked practice field, in the open area behind Matthews Junior High. The practice field was a poorly marked, sparse grass lot that lay between the north side of the school and the Clovis Highway. My shoulder hurt, and I was holding it.

"It's only practice, Lee Roy," I said, looking up at him.

Lee Roy was tall for a ninth grader, maybe over six feet. He was a little pudgy, just some, but he was losing that pudginess from childhood, and you could see that he would be muscular and quick and big. Even with his helmet on, I could see that look that came over him sometimes—a wildness that he had during actual contests.

Lee Roy looked down at me as if he didn't know me. He stared down, and then he seemed to recognize me.

"There's no such thing as practice, Davey," he said. "We gotta play now like we're gonna play Friday night, under the lights."

"Hey!" The ninth-grade coach yelled from across the field. Coach Carson wore a straw hat, and he held a clipboard in front of him wherever he went. His broad belly bulged under his red cotton shirt and served as a fulcrum for the clipboard. When he wasn't listening, some of the boys said that Coach had once played in the National Football League, but none of them were sure about that. It was just something they said, but only when they knew he couldn't hear them.

Lee Roy shook his head and then he was smiling again, the way he did when he met a person for the first time or saw an old friend. The way he did when the fires that burned inside him subsided somewhat. He reached his hand down to me and helped me up, and things were better. But my shoulder still hurt.

"Hey, Buddy, you okay?" Lee Roy said. Now he was suddenly and truly concerned about me—that he had hurt me with that hit. I waved him off. That was just the way Lee Roy was. We started across the practice field to where Coach Carson was holding a school circle with the other boys on the team.

Halfway across the field—I remember it—there was a single football sitting on the fifty-yard line, or thereabouts; it was hard to see the faded white lines on the burned-brown grass of that practice field. Lee Roy stopped there, picked up the ball, and stood for a moment, just holding it in his hand. Then he planted his left foot, strode with his right leg toward the north end of the field, and sailed that football high and far into the air. We all watched it, even Coach Carson. The ball landed with a small puff of dust in the middle of the end zone. It was something, the way Lee Roy threw that ball.

"Wow!" I said. We just stood there on the fifty-yard line. "Wow," I said again. "Someday you're going to throw something big, Lee Roy," I said.

"I think so, too, Davey," said Lee Roy softly, as I remember. It was almost like he was looking into the future, his future. "I think I will throw a big one someday, Davey," he said.

"Hey!" Coach Carson yelled again. We quickly joined the gathering circle of our teammates.

When the practice was over, Lee Roy placed his arm around my shoulder. "Davey, let's get going," he said. "I don't want to miss the next episode of *Sea Hunt* on TV."

He was so friendly the way he did things like that. He could make things well with you, the way he put his arm around you. He could get you to do things his way, and you didn't actually see that it was his way. He was the kind of boy that you could believe in.

We walked home together, which was the way most students did it in those days. No one ever even thought of asking family for a ride, and we wouldn't have gotten a ride if we had asked. Sometimes Cecil Puryear walked with us, and sometimes Jerry Singleton. But Lee Roy and I always walked home together.

As we walked, we kept to the narrow shoulders of the gravel roads that branched out in several directions from the sidewalk perimeter of Matthews Junior High. Lubbock had not felt the economic surges that had swept many parts of the country after World War II. Out on the Southern Plains, it remained a town of simple, crisscrossed streets, with diagonal parking and red-brick paving on Broadway. Residential streets were still mostly dirt and gravel.

Lee Roy wore his glasses when we walked home. He didn't wear them in practice, because he didn't want Coach Carson to know that he needed them. At least, I think that was the reason. Lee Roy never actually said anything about that. In later years, I wondered if Lee Roy wouldn't have been a better football player if he had worn his glasses—you know, able to see the ball better. But I never brought it up around him.

Lee Roy scanned the gravel as we walked. He was always looking for things.

"You got to know the ground, Davey," he said, peering carefully at the stones. "You got to watch the ground carefully. There's luck in the dirt, you know."

I usually walked a little behind Lee Roy. It just felt better that way for both of us. I was kind of a quiet boy, and that fit well with Lee Roy because he could tell me things as we walked, and there wouldn't be all the complications of wondering whose turn it was to say something next. It was just the way it was.

"Last night I was watching the ground careful, and I found a quarter," said Lee Roy. He didn't look back at me. He assumed I was listening, and I was. You can learn a lot from people just by listening to what they say.

"Now that was luck," said Lee Roy. "Finding that quarter, I mean. It was one of those quarters with the Liberty statue on it." He shook his head just at the memory of it. "You know that's got to be lucky.

"But luck doesn't just fall on people, Davey," continued Lee Roy as he scanned the dusty gravel. "You gotta make luck come to you," he said.

I agreed. I walked along behind or to the side of Lee Roy, and I agreed with most of the things he said.

"I saw that cheerleader, Danelle Davis, watching you last game, Lee Roy," I said.

I said this right from behind, up and over Lee Roy's shoulder, so he would definitely hear it.

Lee Roy blushed, and he kept his head down so no one could see. Not that there was anyone there really to see it, except himself and me.

"What do you say about that?" I kept at it, jabbing Lee Roy a little with the words. That was probably wrong, but sometimes I just did that to him.

"I want to be a jet pilot when I'm grown," said Lee Roy. He was changing the subject. He looked up in the sky, hoping to see a plane, but there was none.

"Like Steve Canyon," he said. He stopped here, and turned to me by the side of the road. "I want to fly the jets for our country," he said. It was to say something emphatic that he would stop walking and turn around to tell me something.

Lee Roy looked a little like the comic strip character Steve Canyon, I thought. Tall, crew cut, very intense. But a little pudgier than I thought Steve would be if he were real.

"What're you gonna be, Davey?" he asked. "When you grow up, I mean." He stood facing me, with his hands on his hips.

It occurred to me that Steve Canyon did not wear glasses, either, but I didn't say it. I hadn't really thought about such things that much. It was always much easier to follow Lee Roy's ideas than to think for yourself about hard things like the future.

"I love this country, Davey," he said, still standing, turned around and facing me there on the side of that road in Lubbock. We were fourteen years old. And he meant it.

"Me too," I said. It wasn't much, but that's what I said.

I looked out across the tumbleweed fields around us, fields holding ragged edges against the neighborhood rows of small wooden houses that were moving into them. Lee Roy, too, looked out across the fields. In the distance we could see the oil pumpers far out, beyond the tumbleweeds, where the circular cotton fields lay shimmering at sunset. The pumpers arced slowly up and down, each at a different speed, all out of rhythm, and it looked as if they were great steel anteaters, pushing their noses slowly down into the earth. Across the heat and the dryness of the air, the faint, sulfurous odor of the gases from the wells was present.

Lee Roy smiled. He removed his hands from his hips.

"Okay, Davey," said Lee Roy. "Do you want to race to the sidewalk of my house?"

He did not wait to hear the answer, but whirled and took off running, his book bag clanking against his shoulder. I took one immediate lunge and step, and then I stopped and continued walking, because I didn't like to race when I knew I would lose.

Ahead, on the wooden-frame porch of the Herron house, Lee Roy's mother, Lorea, waited for him. She was always there for Lee Roy when we walked home, standing on the porch, as if she knew when we would be coming. Lingering partly in the shadows, a cotton apron over her cotton dress, Lorea always held a white plastic plate and a clear plastic cup. Cookies and lemonade for Lee Roy.

Lee Roy stopped running short of the walkway to his house. He turned and waved at me as he opened a pine-board gate.

"Hello, Lee Roy," said Lorea, as he cleared the two wooden steps to the porch in a single stride. She always said the same thing. She held out the lemonade and cookies. She and Lee Roy did it the same way each day after football practice. Lee Roy and his mother, they understood each other.

Lee Roy set his book bag down on a swinging porch chair, and he took the cookies and lemonade. He stood next to his mother while he ate, and they did not talk much. They had a way about this, and the way they did it was right for both of them without it having to be discussed.

"Your father will be waiting for you over at the gas station," said Lorea.

"Yes, Ma," said Lee Roy.

I passed by their corner and turned two blocks to the east toward my house. Then I paused at the next corner, looked back, and waved at Lee Roy, still chewing his cookies and standing next to his mother.

Later that evening, after the sun had set and the first hints of cool night air arrived, Lee Roy Herron and his sister, Jane, cleared dishes from the table. They set things in neat stacks in the kitchen, on the tiles next to the sink. Lorea washed everything carefully and set things on a wire drying rack on the other side of the sink. Lee Roy's father, Roy, sat in the living room, in the small space across from the table, reading the *Lubbock Avalanche-Journal*, still wearing a blue denim shirt with the name of the family service station, "Herron's Service."

The Herron family did everything the same way each evening. No one had to say anything. It was just the way they did it.

Later, Lee Roy and Jane took turns taking showers in the house's single bathroom, which was down the hallway, past the kitchen. Afterward, the children went to their rooms, two small bedrooms, side by side, on the other side of the kitchen and near the garage. They studied in their rooms until it was time for bed. They had done it this way from the time they had been little, and now that they were growing up, no one saw fit to change it.

At nine, Lorea came to the bedroom door to turn out Lee Roy's light. She did not always come into his room, but this night he was sitting up in bed, awake. Lorea stepped inside and sat down in the wooden rocker near the door. She could see that Lee Roy had something troubling him.

He did not say anything right away. At age fourteen Lee Roy suddenly looked large to Lorea, as he sat up against the sparse wooden frame of his single bed. She wondered for a moment how her baby with the big blue eyes, the curious look at everything in the world as it came to him, and the always-present smile—how her baby could have grown up so quickly. He had been her pal around the house, following her from room to room and asking her questions about how the smallest things in the world worked, and she would answer the questions, but then that time had passed. She felt a wave of sadness about it all pass through her, and then she closed her eyes and let the sadness pass.

Lee Roy took off his glasses, folded them carefully, and set them on the pine table next to his bed.

"I don't wear those glasses during football, Ma," said Lee Roy. He looked at his mother, and she rocked in the chair and she said nothing.

"I wear them in school, like the doctor said," said Lee Roy, "but in football Coach Carson says glasses don't make the difference." He was trying to state the facts fairly here, so he could hear clearly what his mother had to say about it. He wasn't saying that exactly, of course, but they both understood.

"Of course," he added, "I'm not exactly sure Coach knows I'm supposed to wear glasses, but he probably does, because he talks about it sometimes with us."

Lorea continued to rock.

"Coach says on the field it's not seeing with your eyes that counts." Lee Roy was explaining something, and sometimes, Lorea knew, you had to listen carefully to understand what he was explaining, especially when something was important. "Coach says that it's the feel of the game that counts. Knowing where the ball is, that has to be by the feel of it."

Lorea was listening.

"Coach says that what counts out there is knowing the one thing that you got to do that day. The one thing that's important."

Lorea looked out the window for something, but it was dark. She looked out the window into the night, and she tried to see what lay ahead for her boy. But she could not.

"Coach says none of us have to wear glasses on the football field," said Lee Roy again, softer now as he finished the sentence, finished what he was saying.

Lorea spoke now. It was just the way they did it when they talked at bedtime, and they had always done it this way.

"You don't have to wear the glasses on the football field," she said, and then she stood up and turned out the light.

Far away, in one of the row-house neighborhoods of East Orange, New Jersey, the Stoppiello family stood in the rear of the vestry of Saint Mary's Church. Their eight-year-old son, Frank, hesitated, standing close to his father's side. His father knelt down and placed his arm around the boy's shoulder. Together they looked down the center aisle of the church, at the tinted lights dancing across the backs of empty pews, and at the knave of the church where Father Tormay waited for Frank and the several other children who were to receive their first Communion this day.

"It is the right thing, Frankie," said his father, kneeling next to him so his words came softly against his son's ear. The boy still hesitated. "You can do it, Frankie," said his father again. "You can go up there."

And Frankie walked away from his father and mother, who were proud of him, and who stood close to each other as they watched him walk up the aisle to where Father Tormay was waiting for him.

Frankie was a good boy, his parents thought. They didn't need to say it. Frankie was a good boy.

[4]
1961–1963
Ask Not What Your Country Can Do for You

It was a good time to be young in America, the early sixties.
John Fitzgerald Kennedy was president. He didn't wear a hat,
even if it was cold or windy, and he didn't have gray hair. He put
his hands in his suit-coat pockets when he talked, just like I did,
with the only suit I had. He had a good-looking wife, and you
couldn't help but have the feeling that maybe the two of them
still got it on. With Eisenhower and Mamie, it had required too
great an imagination to conceive of something like that. We felt
good about JFK's politics, too, because we were still Democrats
in Texas at that time. We were the populist kind of Democrats,
and we liked it when the president faced down the steel barons
and made them roll back prices and called them "Sons of Business." America seemed to rule the world with our auto industry,
our B-52 bombers, and the New York Yankees. It seemed, if you
were sixteen, that anything was possible. Later we learned that
the president was a philanderer, big time, that he had been out-
smarted by the Russians over the Cuban missiles more than we
knew, and that he had probably been wrong about how to approach Vietnam. But we didn't know all that in the early sixties.
To us at Lubbock High School then it seemed like anything was
possible.

Lee Roy Herron [top center, wearing glasses, with hand tucked under his arm] and David Nelson [wearing plaid shirt] stand shoulder to shoulder in a 1962 National Honor Society gathering at Lubbock High School. Courtesy of Lubbock High School.

I had part-time jobs in those years, and I was saving money. Every time I got paid, I deposited some in a savings account that my father had opened for me in the Lubbock National Bank. In 1961 I worked washing dishes at the Top of the Plains Restaurant, on the twentieth floor of the Great Plains Life Insurance Building. (Later, when the tornado of 1970 came, the Life Insurance Building was bent right over, so that afterward it made people dizzy to look up at it. But it didn't fall.) I worked forty-eight hours a week that summer, and I saved money so I could buy a Cushman Eagle motor scooter, a black one. My favorite thing about the Top of the Plains job was that I got to work Saturday afternoons alone, cleaning up and closing. I really liked that—the solitude of it, I think. I put nickels in the jukebox, played "Sea of Love" by Phil Phillips, and had the place to myself.

With the Cushman Eagle, I could ride to Lubbock High from our house on Fifteenth Street, a distance of about four miles. I did that for three years. When it snowed or rained, which it didn't often do in Lubbock, I got cold and wet.

What I liked about the Cushman wasn't the status of it. It was that I could come to school my own way, when I wanted to come. I could leave when I wanted to leave. And no one had given it to me. For some reason, I have always had a problem with people giving things to me.

Lee Roy was there, too. He had become a natural leader at Lubbock High by then. He knew a lot of people, and he always smiled when he met them in the hall. He could remember their names, which was something I couldn't do too well. I don't think he was faking it with the smile, either. I think he really liked a lot of those people. And it wasn't just the cool kids that elicited Lee Roy's smiles. He even liked the kids we called greasers, not that we had many of them, and Mexican Americans. Lee Roy ran for office in the Lubbock High School class of 1963, and he won every time. He was elected vice president in the tenth grade, and president in eleventh and twelfth. But Lee Roy was changing, and there were other sides to him back then, which I didn't see well at the time. Looking back, I can see them. Lee Roy and I always talked, and he told me about things, but at the time it was hard to know what was important and what was not. I can remember them now, some of the things he told me.

August 1, 1961

"Dad," said Lee Roy. "If I open the gas station tomorrow, and work it all day, do you think I could have the evening off?"

Lee Roy and his father were standing in the small office part of the Herron gas station. There was a counter on one side, cluttered with papers and with a cash register at one end, the mechanical type from the National Cash Register Corporation, the kind whose buttons you had to push really hard to make the wafer-thin plastic numbers pop up in the glass window at the top. If you hit the buttons wrong, sometimes the numbers would only go halfway up and get stuck, and then the drawer wouldn't open.

"These summer days are our busy days, Lee Roy," said his

father. His dad wore overalls, with a denim shirt under them, and the generations of oil and dust that had caked and slimed and stained the fabrics had combined so that the shirt and the overalls were all one thing—or looked to be so. It was as if Lee Roy's father wore one oil-blue outfit with two shoulder straps and brass fittings.

"I know, Dad, but . . ." And here it was awkward, and Lee Roy was making sure that he said what had to be said, so his father would understand. "I have a date with Martha Cates for tomorrow night." That was it. Lee Roy rested his case there.

Lee Roy's dad was a quiet man. You could tell by looking at him that he was hardworking, and he spoke quietly, as if he was shy. Looking back on it now, I think maybe he *was* shy. I liked hearing his voice, though. It was soft, and it had a kind of soothing hum to it. He was different from Lee Roy.

Lee Roy's father sat down on one of the two plastic chairs in the office. One of them had a broken back. Both pitched and yawed considerably when you sat in them. There was a small table between them, with old copies of *Life* magazine strewn about.

"OK, Lee Roy," said his father. But he did not look at Lee Roy when he said it.

"Don't worry, Dad," said Lee Roy. "I won't let you down. I'll hustle so much business tonight that you could just shut the station down tomorrow night and come out even!"

Lee Roy was relieved. He smiled. "Here comes a car now!" said Lee Roy, and he bolted from behind the counter to head out for business. He paused with the glass door still in his hand and looked at his father.

"How is that car of yours running, Lee Roy?" asked his father. Lee Roy looked out the door. Parked by the two garage bays was a black 1952 Chevrolet, with protruding nose. Six cylinders in line and three speeds forward if you could jerk and jiggle the steering column shift lever so that it would go into the right place. He and his father had worked on it together. It was Lee Roy's car.

"Okay, I guess," said Lee Roy. And so it was. His father didn't need to say anything more.

The next night Lee Roy picked up Martha Cates at her house, driving the black Chevy.

Martha lived in the Rush neighborhood, too, not far from my house. I didn't date much in high school, however, and she was popular. *Very* popular. By this time, Lee Roy's family had moved to a red-brick house on Parkway Drive, on the northeast side of Lubbock, so Lee Roy had to drive about a mile or two to get to our neighborhood.

Martha walked out of the house as Lee Roy drove up. She wore a linen skirt with a buckle across the back, and loafer-like shoes that the girls called flats. Martha was slender, tall, and beautiful. Her hair was black and her eyes were dark. Later she would be known as Marcie Johnston, and then for a time another last name through a second marriage. But she would always look the same. She spent her whole life in Lubbock until she died of a brain tumor in the early years of the twenty-first century, and she always looked beautiful, and people always liked her.

"Hello, Lee Roy," she said, as he held the passenger door open for her.

"Hello, Martha," said Lee Roy. As he walked around the back of the car to enter the driver's side, Lee Roy wondered if men ever really got comfortable, at ease, with the girls they knew and dated. He had his doubts.

It was at the end of the day, and the light was fading. They drove to the Golden Horseshoe Drive-In. The movie that night was *The Guns of Navarone*, starring Gregory Peck.

Lee Roy parked the Chevrolet on the right-hand side of one of the stations in the lot. Each station had two speakers—heavy, gray, steel, cylindrical things—one side smooth, and one side grooved, where the sound came out. The speakers had curved hooks that fit over the window edge of a car door. You couldn't go to the drive-in if it was cold, because you had to have the window down, at least on the driver's side, for the speakers to work in the car.

The Golden Horseshoe also had drive-in food service, and you could order through the speaker, when it first came on, and the girls who worked there would bring trays of hamburgers and malts, the trays hooking onto passenger-side car doors.

Martha ordered a chicken sandwich and a Coke. Lee Roy ordered a cheeseburger and a vanilla malted. He always ordered that. In fact, that summer of 1961, Lee Roy went to the same movie over and over.

The film began—the fictionalized story of six somewhat dysfunctional soldiers parachuting into Greece behind enemy lines in World War II, to destroy the German gun emplacement at Navarone. Lee Roy wasn't exactly sure if there was a place called Navarone, but he loved the movie. Afterward, he and Martha went to the White Pig, a little drive-in restaurant on Fourth Street, where you could get the same kinds of things they served at the local Hi-D-Ho drive-ins, but at the White Pig it was usually less noisy.

"Why do you always want to see the same movie, Lee Roy?" asked Martha, after they had sat down at one of the white tables. "What is it about *The Guns of Navarone?*"

"I just like it," said Lee Roy.

"You can't say 'I just like it,'" said Martha. "We're becoming adults now. You've got to have a reason for why you do things," she said.

"I like it that those guys did something big, something important for their country," said Lee Roy.

"But it was very violent," said Martha. "They did something very violent."

Lee Roy now sat forward, just a little. "You can't call that violent, Martha," he said. "Doing something to save your country is not violent."

"But they killed all those people," said Martha. "How about that?" Martha was thoughtful, even at that stage in her life.

"They were Germans," said Lee Roy. "They were the enemy."

"The Bible does not say, 'Thou shalt not kill except for your enemies,'" said Martha. "It says just 'Thou shalt not kill.'" Martha was religious then and throughout her life. No one ever doubted her faith. It was a part of her.

Lee Roy thought about that one. The stern formalism of his parents' church had never seemed incompatible with killing the enemy, to Lee Roy at least. But the way Martha had put it, the way the words of the commandments were so straightforward, that was something to consider.

"Also," said Martha, "did you see that they all died on their mission, except for Gregory Peck and that one other guy?"

Lee Roy thought that one over. It was true what Martha was saying, but to Lee Roy it was all so heroic, the way the Allied soldiers had moved out against that German gun.

"If you're a soldier," said Lee Roy, "that's just what you have to do. You have to be prepared to die for your country." Here he was strong, emphatic, and clear.

"Oh, well," said Martha. "I suspect the time of the wars is over. We're just too dominant in the world," she finished. Then, as Lee Roy was about to say something himself, she added, "And if nuclear war comes with the Russians, that won't be war like *The Guns of Navarone*, or like anything else we've ever seen. That will just be blowing people up."

Lee Roy let things rest here, and he turned the topic to other things in the life of high school students in the early 1960s.

August 2, 1961

Lee Roy was competitive. Sometimes this made him do strange things.

Sometimes after my job, if Lee Roy was off early from the gas station, we would play tennis on the public courts in Lubbock, a few of which were located next to some of the numerous playa lakes inside the city limits. Bill Cox, Jr., sometimes came too, after he was done with his hours at the Furr's Supermarket. One time, I remember, Bill and Lee Roy were playing, and I was sitting on the metal bleachers to the side, waiting to play the winner. Usually Lee Roy won, whether he was playing me or Bill. It was an expectation we all had. But one night Bill won the first set. I was sitting there, watching, and I thought for sure Lee Roy would recover and win, as he almost always did—and Lee Roy was trying his best. But Bill kept hitting the shots, including some really hard backhands past Lee Roy, streaking on a line under the summer lights of the court, and Bill won. Both Bill and I paused, and we waited to see what would happen. Lee Roy stood still, transfixed too. Then he picked up his tennis racket, walked to the edge of the court where it met a playa lake, and heaved the racket as far into the lake as he could. And that was pretty far.

We had all read *The Once and Future King* in high school, and I can assure you that there was no Lady of the Lake in the playa to help out—Lee Roy's racket disappeared into the dark waters, not to rise again. Afterward, I always wondered if he ever told his father about that, or how something had happened to his tennis racket, but I never asked Lee Roy about that.

August 3, 1961

A man came into the office at the Herron gas station. It was after dark. A slow night at the station. Hot and still and clear in the Texas summer, with the edge of orange from the daytime sky still visible out to the west. Lee Roy was working the evening hours at the station alone.

"Evening," said Lee Roy. The man seemed a little tense. Like something was wrong—or would be wrong soon.

"You alone here?" asked the stranger.

Lee Roy focused his attention a little more carefully on the man. He was an Anglo. Maybe on the young side. Unshaven.

"Yup," said Lee Roy.

"You got some money in that cash register?" said the man. He nodded toward the counter between them.

Lee Roy felt his teeth come together strongly. "Why?" he asked.

"Cuz I want it," said the man.

"You can't have any of my father's money," said Lee Roy. Lee Roy didn't feel it as anger. He felt it as evil outside himself—in this man with the low-slung jeans and the bulky white T-shirt. Lee Roy felt a rising of energy and intensity, felt it going toward this man who stood there in front of him and threatened his father's livelihood. He told me afterward that was how he felt.

"Give it all to me. Now!" said the man. He had his hand in the side pocket of his jeans, and he pulled out a folding knife, the switchblade kind that flicks open when you push the stainless steel clasp on the side. He switched it open.

Lee Roy saw only something out there that had to be done. His right hand was already on the handle of the thirty-two-inch Hillerich & Bradsby baseball bat that leaned against the corner of the counter. He picked it up and held it high. "No one gets my father's money," he said.

There was a pause, a short hiatus in sound and movement there in the office of the Herron gas station. And then it was over. The man reached up with his left hand and closed the knife. He put the knife back in his pocket and he left the office.

Lee Roy told me about it the next night, when we were sitting on the bleachers at the tennis court. I couldn't believe what he had done.

"Lee Roy," I said. "What were you thinking?"

"I wasn't thinking," said Lee Roy. "It was wrong, what he was trying to do."

"Yes," I said. "But what about the knife? Weren't you afraid?"

"No," said Lee Roy. "I didn't feel afraid." Even now, a day later, he did not seem terribly aroused by it. I would have been shaking, I think. I probably would have given the man the money. That's what the sheriff said you were supposed to do, when he had come to talk to our civics class. But that wasn't what Lee Roy had done.

"You could have been hurt, Lee Roy," I said. "It's only money. You could have just given it to him."

"No, Davey," he said. "It was wrong, what he was trying to do. My father works real hard for his money, and it was wrong for that man to walk into the station and try to steal it."

It was hard to know what to say to that. I turned away, looking out over the little lake there. I wondered where Lee Roy's tennis racquet was. I wondered what I would have done in the gas station situation. I really wondered—what if I had been tested like that? I already suspected that, before it's done, life tests us all. Life tests us all.

"Were you prepared to kill that guy with the baseball bat?" I looked back at Lee Roy. I really wondered.

"I don't know, Davey," he said. "That's not what I was thinking, with the bat and all. I wasn't thinking I was going to kill him, or hurt him. I was just thinking what he was trying to do was wrong, and I was going to make something happen to stop it."

And that was the end of it. We never did discuss that incident again, and I didn't think of it again until many years later.

I did notice something a little over the top about Lee Roy a year after his foiling the robbery attempt.

It was the fall of 1962, we were seniors at Lubbock High, and the Cuban Missile Crisis was in progress. Of course we didn't know it by that name then, and the facts about what was happening were hazy, but it seemed that a military confrontation was occurring such as had not been seen since World War II, when we were infants.

At the peak of the crisis, President Kennedy placed a shipping embargo on Cuba and stated that all ships coming into Cuban territorial waters would be searched by the U.S. Navy. Russian cruisers were reported to be in the area. Lee Roy came up to me during this time, after lunch in the cafeteria, but before the fifth hour of classes had begun. He was positively elated.

"Have you heard? Davey, have you heard?" he said.

"What?" I said, but I knew what Lee Roy was talking about.

The missiles in Cuba—the sending of U.S. destroyers and cruisers, the embarkation of a battalion of marines from Camp Lejeune, North Carolina. I'm not sure Lee Roy actually knew what a battalion of marines was, but he was excited about it.

"We've embargoed Cuba!" he shouted. "The president is sending the marines! We're going to search all ships. The Russians are going to have to"—and here he paused and turned his head to make sure we were alone in the hall—"kiss our asses now!"

I had not seen Lee Roy so hyper before. Not that I could remember. And I had almost never heard him use a coarse expression like "kiss my ass." Even when he threw the tennis racket in the lake he didn't talk like that.

"Lee Roy," I said, "this is bad stuff, the embargo and the navy and all that." I had been following the news, too, of course—everybody was at that time.

"Embargoes can be considered acts of war," I said. "That's what Mrs. Hawkins says." Mrs. Hawkins was our history teacher. We had been able to talk of little else in history class that fall. The scheduled curriculum got blown away by the real events covered on radio and television.

"War," said Lee Roy. There seemed some gratification or satisfaction in his voice, the way he said that word. "Maybe we can finally get a chance to teach those Russians a lesson or two." He was savoring it—the word and the thought of war.

"Lee Roy," I said. I was uncomfortable with the whole thing. Everything was getting messed up here, even history class. "War—do you know what that would mean if we got into a war with the Russians?"

"Yeah," said Lee Roy. "It would mean that those Russians might get a chance to meet the Marine Corps."

The bell rang for the fifth-hour classes, and we had to move on. I wanted to serve the country too, but I wasn't so sure about what was right as Lee Roy was. I just wasn't sure.

The missile crisis smoothed over, and life went on. We finished high school in the summer of 1963, and both Lee Roy and I enrolled in Texas Tech University as freshmen that fall. I don't think either of us ever thought about going somewhere else for college. Tech was right there in Lubbock, and we could save money by living at home for the first year or two, and that's just what everybody did.

Lee Roy said he wanted to major in government at Texas Tech, and I studied pre-law courses. I liked the books, and I figured lawyers would have plenty of books. Besides, law was a secure field. You wouldn't have to worry about a job if you were a lawyer. We both worked pretty hard at our studies that first semester and were both going to be inducted into the honor fraternity at Texas Tech, Phi Eta Sigma. Lee Roy and I were in the top 2.25 percent of our freshman class academically. Everything seemed to be going well.

Then in November the president was assassinated in Dallas, and it changed things. Everything was a little different afterward—more than just that one man was dead and another, a Texan, had become president. Partly it was because of the way things had happened that weekend. President Kennedy had been shot at midday on Friday and then everything in the country just seemed to pause. High school basketball games were canceled in Lubbock, as were the sock hops afterward. We all sat in front of our television sets on Saturday and Sunday, or we listened to the radio.

Lee Harvey Oswald was shot to death on live television on

Sunday morning that weekend. I wasn't watching because I had gotten tired of the television, but Lee Roy called me up right away, said what had happened, and told me to turn my television set back on. They didn't have instant replays then, and we were probably the better for it that Sunday morning in 1963. All that happened that weekend didn't seem to fit with the way things were supposed to be.

After that weekend, we still had to return to class, homework still had to be done, the guys who were the dorks at Texas Tech were still the dorks. But something wasn't right after that. It made us feel that maybe America wasn't really completely in charge of things as much as we had thought. This is how I felt, and I know Lee Roy felt the same way, because we talked about things. Both of us started to think about how we might join the military.

I don't remember too much else from that time until the end of our freshman year, the summer of 1964, when Lee Roy and I talked more about the future. Again, as was often the case, Lee Roy was the leader here, and I was walking a step or two behind him.

"This'll be my last summer working the gas station," said Lee Roy. We were sitting, as we often did, in the first row of the metal bleachers at the lighted tennis court by the playa lake. It was an early evening in June, and we were just talking.

"How so?" I asked.

"I'm gonna join the marines, Davey!" His eyes lit up, even in the reflected light of the Texas sunset, like they had that afternoon two years before, during the Cuban Missile Crisis. I didn't need to say anything. Yes, I thought. Of course Lee Roy is going to join the marines. It was one of those things that afterward you don't even wonder about it, but seems like it was foretold.

"Ol' Lee Roy Herron of Lubbock, Texas, is going to be a

marine!" He leaned forward. He looked at me with eagerness in his eyes. It made me uncomfortable. I said nothing.

"And not just a marine, Davey," he continued. "An officer. A marine officer," he said. Then he sat back on the aluminum bench.

"How?" I asked.

"They have a program called the 'PLC' program, short for 'Platoon Leaders Class.' You go to two six-week summer camps during college, and then you're commissioned as a second lieutenant at graduation. A second lieutenant in the marines, Davey!"

Lee Roy savored it. He felt good about it. He wasn't done explaining it. He knew all the details of it.

"You can also go to one ten-week course at Quantico, instead of the two six-weeks. You get the same commission at college graduation."

Lee Roy looked directly at me, and I had a bad feeling about what was coming.

"That's what you should do, Davey," he said. "The ten-week PLC camp."

Definitely I had a bad feeling about it.

"I don't know, Lee Roy," I said. Fortunately, Lee Roy was back into his own fantasies about the Marine Corps officer thing.

"The reason it's better to do the two six-week camps is that you get an earlier 'pay entry base date,' for your pay and all. The amount of money you get in the marines depends upon your rank, and on that pay entry base date. The earlier the base date is in time, the more money you get. The officer selection officer in Dallas explained that to me."

I was trying to think this through. Here we were, sitting in the evening heat of the Texas summer, looking out across the small lake in front of us, and Lee Roy was explaining how he was going to make more money by shipping himself off to Quantico now, rather than later. The Marine Corps was not my idea of how to make money, pay entry base date or no.

"How did you meet an officer selection officer from Dallas?" I asked.

"I didn't have to go to Dallas," said Lee Roy. "The OSO—that's what they call 'em—comes to Tech once a year, to explain things to students, you know. He had a table outside the library in the spring. Didn't you see it?"

"No," I said.

"You should have seen the uniform he had on, Davey." Here Lee Roy was moved, deeply intent on explaining this matter.

"It wasn't that it was that colorful or anything, Davey," he continued. "The marines have colorful uniforms, but the OSO wore only this khaki garrison uniform, with a tie, black buttons, and a coat."

I was trying to picture it in my mind's eye.

"It was a fighting man's uniform, Davey," said Lee Roy. This was the point for Lee Roy. Here, he had said what it was. I was worried that Lee Roy might grab me, lift me up from the bleachers, and heave me into the playa lake like the tennis racket.

"I'd like to see it," I said, mostly so Lee Roy wouldn't pick me up from the bench.

"Better than that, Davey," he said, calmer now, satisfied. "You should see the OSO next year when he comes."

I thought about it. I was trying to picture it all.

"You would have gone to the Naval Academy if you could have got in, Davey," said Lee Roy. That was true. I had been nominated as principal candidate to the Academy in high school, but the nomination hadn't really gone anywhere, because I wore glasses, and the Naval Academy didn't allow glasses. I had thought about West Point, where you could wear glasses, but it just hadn't seemed right.

"You should join the PLC, too, Davey," continued Lee Roy. He had a way about him, Lee Roy. I looked out at the flat surface of the playa lake and I wondered where Lee Roy's tennis racquet was, lying out there, somewhere in its depths. And here was Lee Roy, trying to convince me to join the marines. There was something to it. It was a little preposterous, but Lee Roy could make things seem possible.

And that following spring, true to his word, Lee Roy did arrange for me to meet the Marine Corps Officer Selection Officer from Dallas, when he came to visit Texas Tech.

And early in my junior year of college, at Texas Tech University, I said that I would do it. I said that I would go to Quantico for the ten-week Platoon Leaders Class program, in the summer of 1966.

I don't know why I did that, but I did it.

[5]

1966

To Be an Officer of Men

Monday, June 13, 1966

Texas Tech University

Lubbock, Texas

"Are you going then, David?" asked Lee Roy.

I remember him saying that. I remember standing there, wondering myself if I was going.

Lee Roy and I stood just inside the swinging doors of the Gaston Hall dormitory at Texas Tech. I remember the coolness of the old air conditioners, humming and clanking and dripping condensation along the window edges inside the building. Outside was the summer heat, the heat of the South; Lee Roy and I would be going out in it, and once we went out those doors there would be no easy return. I wanted to hold onto that coolness for one more moment. I looked through the glass to the gray airport bus waiting outside.

"'Cuz I'm going, and the bus is here now, and it's time," Lee Roy said.

Of course Lee Roy was going to get on the bus. It would be his second six-week PLC camp at Quantico. He had been there before. But I was going to do the ten-week camp, and I had not gone before. Charles Lance was also going to the airport, by car. There would be three of us in the PLC program from Texas Tech. Things around me seemed to float in space. I felt that I was standing still and the world was swimming around me. I had a bad feeling about it all.

The coolness of the dormitory felt good. Even Lee Roy hesitated before he went out into that heat. We could both see the squat Greyhound bus idling outside with its door swung open. It would take us to the Lubbock airport, where we would board an aircraft to Washington, D.C., and beyond that ride other buses to the Platoon Leaders Class training camps at Quantico, Virginia.

I never did much like the Lubbock airport. There was always too much of a bustle there for me. I was someone who liked to be grounded. To this day, I prefer to drive by car whenever I go back to Lubbock.

"The bus is waiting," said Lee Roy.

"I'm going," I said, because I couldn't think of how I'd explain it to myself if I didn't go.

The door clanked open, swinging out into the bright light of the West Texas summer. Two young women walked in—bouffant hair, blue eyes, books, and miniskirts. They smiled at us. They walked on by, and neither of us turned to watch. Lee Roy stepped forward, caught the swinging door before it closed, and held it open. I picked up my valise and we were out, across that threshold.

June 14–15, 1966

Marine Corps Base, Quantico
Camp Upshur

Entering the PLC camp that day in June of 1966 was like riding an escalator down through the rings of Dante's inferno. The flight to the old Washington National Airport hadn't been that bad, but I'd felt so tight in my stomach that I couldn't eat breakfast. There were enlisted marines waiting for us at the airport, wearing summer khaki uniforms, dark-green stripes on their sleeves, and medals above their left breast pockets. We were checked off on clipboards and placed on waiting buses, and then the buses rolled south, across the rising ground of northern Virginia. We passed through the main gate of the Quantico Marine Corps base, and there at the entrance was the huge bronze statue of the flag-raising on Iwo Jima, the larger-than-life-size squad of marines bent on their task of seating the flag on the rocky hillside, leaning into the unseen winds of war around them. We all looked at that statue as guards waved the buses in. No one talked as we rolled down the asphalt road inside the base.

There was a golf course there, just inside the base, strung out along rolling grounds above the Potomac River. I remember looking at the young men pulling golf carts along landscaped fairways, and even though I didn't play golf, I remember thinking that those guys were among the most blessed in the entire world because they were there—while we were on buses headed for the camps in the hills. The golfers stopped when our buses rolled by, and they stood looking up at us, and I did not like the way it felt. We were headed for Camp Upshur, an outpost of steel Quonset huts in the Virginia hills, where generations of marine officers had begun their journey to war. The bus turned up the hillsides, and trees grew thick along the edges of the road.

Much later I lay awake in my squad bay bunk. I had not slept a moment. I don't believe I had even dared to close my eyes, and it was now near dawn on Tuesday morning, I could tell by the sickly gray feeling in my stomach. I remember the day and the date, and I think I always will. It was June 14, 1966.

I lay awake in the bunk with another officer candidate above me, and rows of pairs of others up and down the concrete floor of the building. There was almost no sound inside, not even snoring, and I figured almost everyone else was silently awake like me.

I lay still and tense, almost at attention, the way the sergeant instructor had said when he had turned out the lights six hours before. Six hours and no sleep. No rest. I remember a fear I had, that without sleep things might shut down inside me during the day ahead—that I might not be able to make it that day. The thought of not making it was like some terrible and alluring forbidden potion that if tasted of it might cause the thought to come true. I lay with my eyes open in the dark, and I told myself that surely I would get some rest, a few moments of sleep even now at the hour just before dawn. Sleep would come, I told myself. And I did not let myself think about what might happen if it didn't.

I felt I had made a terrible mistake in coming here.

I heard a screen door opening slowly at the end of the squad bay, and saw the helmeted shadow of one of the training sergeants, but it was not the same sergeant instructor as on the previous day. Not looking directly at him, still lying at attention in my rack, I could see that this one was different. This must be the platoon sergeant, I thought. We had heard about him, and now we would meet him. I lay there in the gray light of near dawn, and I was absolutely sure I had made a terrible mistake in coming here.

The screen door slammed. The long chain of neon lights in the center of the ceiling of the squad bay exploded into what seemed the glare of a hundred suns. With a horrendous crash the platoon sergeant sent two steel trash cans down the center aisle of the squad bay, careening against the bunks across the concrete floor. Then came his screams—coarse, guttural screams.

"Get up! Get up! Get up, you shitbirds!" It was not so much a scream as an animal growl, a menacing noise from deep within his throat as he walked slowly down the center of the squad bay. He kicked the horrible garbage cans, the noise was terrifying, and he growled as he passed each pair of bunks.

"Get up, you fucking maggots!" he yelled, and he smacked a carved wooden stick against the metal bars of the bunk frames as he walked, and the aged bunks clanged and groaned.

I was up. Standing at attention by the side of my bunk, or the best imitation of attention that I could muster from war movies I had seen at the Golden Horseshoe an eternity ago. Those times seemed far away now, and suddenly wonderful. How I longed for them at that moment. I will never forget the feeling. When I die, unless it comes too quickly for reflection, I will tell myself that I still feel better than I did that day in 1966.

The platoon sergeant stopped in front of the candidate two bunks short of where I stood. As nearly as I could tell without turning my head to look, that candidate stood straight and tense against the upright bars of his bunk, like me. But even from the side-looking angle of my vision, I could see that this "candidate" had his belly sticking out against the green T-shirts that had been issued the previous day.

The platoon sergeant placed his wooden stick softly against the young man's belly. I had a terrible feeling about what was coming, but at the same time I was almost euphoric that it was not coming to me. And that made me feel worse. My parents had taught me that that was wrong. But here, in this World War II Quonset hut in the back hills of the Quantico base, it was my parents who had been wrong. I was learning things here that would be lessons poorly fitted to the world outside.

"What have we here?" asked the platoon sergeant, pausing in front of the protuberant belly of the candidate. The platoon sergeant was poised statue-like, holding his short wooden stick against the young man's flesh.

"Are you a fucking fat boy?" asked the platoon sergeant, leaning toward the hapless candidate as he spoke, and there was sadism and cruelty in his voice. The candidate did not answer.

"Aren't you in the wrong fucking place?" shouted the platoon sergeant. He was now leaning toward the young man's face, with the metal visor of his helmet threatening the candidate's face like a cutting edge of pain. There was no answer.

"I don't hear you!" screamed the platoon sergeant savagely into the candidate's face. "When I talk to you maggots," and now he stepped back, turned his helmeted head, and scanned the fifty bunks in the squad bay, "and when I ask you a fucking question I expect to hear an answer!" His face had darkened now, and it seemed to me that there was death in this man. I told myself that he was acting, that this was just something he'd been taught to do to impress us. But I had my doubts. I had a very strong feeling that he had killing in him.

Another candidate, standing on the near side of the bunk from the chubby one, stepped into the center of the squad bay and held his hands out as if to protect his bunkmate.

"He'll lose weight, sir," said the second candidate, standing out of the ranks. Looking straight at the platoon sergeant, he held out his hands, hands of compassion, telling the platoon sergeant to stop.

The platoon sergeant seemed too shocked to move for a second. Then a wave of darkness and rage swept over him, and he grabbed the Good Samaritan and swept him across his left leg so that the candidate fell sprawling across the cracked concrete floor.

There was complete silence in the squad bay. From what I could see out of the side of my vision, the Good Samaritan sprawled across the floor looked strong and tall and tough. But there he lay, spread out in shame. I did not like what I saw. I remember thinking that surely there must be rules here—policies, procedures, a book somewhere with pages that say what is right and what is wrong. But everything that was happening—that was real here—said that we were now in a place far from rules and policies. And it was a place of killing. I could feel that in the shadows of what was happening.

The platoon sergeant stood in the center of the squad bay, and he looked at us: fifty PLC candidates, standing one by one in our green shorts and T-shirts. The one on the floor lay still, in shock and surprise. "Get back up," said the platoon sergeant, without actually looking down at him. The candidate on the floor got up and resumed his place next to the bunk, next to the chubby one.

"My name is Staff Sergeant McNab," said the platoon sergeant. He stood calmly now in the center of the squad bay, speaking to all of us. We were relieved that he was talking to us.

"My name is Staff Sergeant P. M. McNab, and you all will come to see that my initials stand for 'Pleasant Moments.' But you will never call me that." I wondered to myself if there was something funny about this, if he was making fun of us in a way. But then I thought no. Even the humor here was dark and violent and killing.

"You will call me 'Platoon Sergeant,' and nothing else," he said. He kept walking, in short, almost prancing steps. His black boots clicked against the hard concrete, and his sateen utility uniform was a deep shade of green against the dawn darkness outside.

"You will not call me 'Sir,' and you will not salute me except for instructional purposes," he said, and he looked to the left and right as he spoke.

Staff Sergeant McNab was moving slowly down the center aisle of the squad bay now. He moved past me, and I could see him straight on, without turning my head. He was not that tall, I thought. Perhaps five foot nine or ten at the most. He had a stocky look, a square look about everything, including his lined face, which was crossed by a thin mustache. His boots made a crisp, cutting sound as he stepped off the center line of the bay. He looked older than he probably was, I thought. He looked like a man who had been through many things.

"I will be your platoon sergeant during your ten weeks here, those of you who make it." Staff Sergeant McNab was explaining things. The rancor was gone from his voice, and now he was explaining the way things were. He had a teaching side to him, I thought. I felt so relieved.

"Those of you who cannot make it will 'drop on request.'" He said these words strongly, savoring them, putting special emphasis on "cannot," as if he prized the word and kept it close at all times. "D-O-R," he said. "Not all of you will become marine officers, and those of you who cannot hack it will D-O-R," he said. When he said the word "hack," he was harsh, cutting, as if those who *could* hack would become cutters of men.

"That means," Sergeant McNab continued, "that you will be able to go home immediately, sit down in a cool room in front of your television set, pull on your peckers, drink Coca-Cola, and eat pizza." He looked at us all. "The rest of you will remain with me." He was at the far end of the squad bay now. He had walked past everyone. Everyone had been close to him, had felt his primitive violence. "And those of you who stay will become officers of men," he said.

Staff Sergeant McNab stopped. He turned. He looked back down the length of the squad bay.

"Anytime," he said. "D-O-R."

He started back toward the center of the squad bay.

As he walked, Staff Sergeant McNab raised his left hand to his helmet, and he removed it to draw his hand across his forehead. It was a mannerism that Sergeant McNab had, one of many, as we would learn. He looked at us. He had a granite, handsome face, with brown hair combed neatly against the crease of the helmet. His face could have come from a *Life* magazine World War II photograph of marines in garrison.

As Sergeant McNab grasped his helmet to replace it, even from my peripheral vision I could see that his left hand was deformed— crippled and scarred. Without acknowledging that anyone had seen it, Staff Sergeant McNab continued his explanations, now about himself.

"Some of you have seen my arm," said Sergeant McNab, nearing the center of the squad bay again, where the garbage cans lay on their sides. His black boots were still clicking rhythmically.

"That happened to me on the road to Koto Ri, in Korea, coming down from the Chosin Reservoir with the 1st Marine Division in 1950," he said. He lowered his head just a little now. I felt that killing wind return to his voice.

"One of the gooners shot me on the road to Koto Ri," he said. He lowered his head more, so the visor of the helmet cut a sharp line above his eyes. I could already tell, instantly and completely, that to this man all Asians were "gooners," that he hated them all, that he probably had spent much of his life killing them, and that he carried deep regrets for the ones he had missed.

"But the man that did that to me is dead," he said. Staff Sergeant McNab stopped. Then he started up again, moving past the center of the bay.

"I killed him," he said. He said it matter-of-factly, as if that had just been his job that day. And then it occurred to me that probably that *had* been his job that day. To Staff Sergeant McNab, that "gooner" had had to be killed, as had many others like him on that day and other days. I wondered, was this going to happen to me? Was I going to become like that, a person who on some day like any other in 1968 or 1969, perhaps, with the sun rising and a warm wind blowing and perhaps a hint of moisture in the air, would get up, have coffee in a tent, go up the next hillside, kill another man, and afterward say that I had killed a "gooner" that day? Something here did not match what the officer selection officer from Dallas had talked about.

"I have fought for this country in three wars," continued Staff Sergeant McNab, coming to a stop about two-thirds of the way down the center of the bay. "The campaigns on Okinawa in World War II, the Chosin Reservoir in Korea, and the Operation Starlight fights around Da Nang in Vietnam last year."

Staff Sergeant McNab stood in the center of the group, and the glare and the hardness was returning to him.

"The gooners don't like me," he said. "The gooners have never liked me," he said.

He carried on. He was going to tell more.

"Last year in Vietnam my platoon commander told me that the people of Vietnam would like me better if I shaved off my mustache, because with the mustache they thought I looked like one of those French pussies. And they hated the French."

McNab paused. We all listened expectantly. I had the feeling again that he was teaching us something, in his way.

"Well, I didn't shave it off," said Sergeant McNab. That was the end of this lesson.

"Now make your bunks, get yourselves into your physical training uniforms, and fall outside the squad bay for morning formation."

SSgt. P. M. McNab walked out the same squad bay door

through which he had entered, and the screen door slammed behind him.

I made it through that day. I slept better the next night. There was something to what Staff Sergeant McNab had said. Something to "if a 'gooner' has to be killed this day, then kill him, so you can move on to the next task." I shortened my time horizon to one day at a time. I tried to take what each day gave, to grasp what came, to learn from it. All that I could control was that, the way I experienced what came each day. And then, paradoxically, I began to feel more and more in charge of things that could not be changed.

There was a rhythm to the days. There was a daily training schedule posted on a small cork board at the end of the squad bay. Each day started with physical training at dawn, followed by formations for breakfast at the mess hall, formations for classes in large, steel-walled classroom buildings, formations for weapons training at distant firing ranges, and cleaning—cleaning rifles, cleaning boots, cleaning heads—toilets—and squad bays until there was neither dust nor rust left anywhere. Everything was in order. Everything was done by the group. There seemed to be no weekends or holidays. Every day was the same. It was definitely more Sparta than Athens, I thought. But I was making it. I was beginning to feel the rhythm of the Marine Corps.

From time to time I thought of Lee Roy, who had been assigned to a different training camp, at the Mainside location of the Quantico base, where the PLC seniors were. We never saw those candidates, and I wondered how Lee Roy was doing with it all. There was little communication with the world outside our camp.

In the second training week the overweight candidate D-O-R'd. At least that's what they told us. One morning he just wasn't there. The sergeant instructor, a noncommissioned officer more junior than Staff Sergeant McNab, with three stripes to McNab's four, told us at formation that the candidate had D-O-R'd because he was a "non-hacker." That was a terrible word, I thought to myself. "Non-hacker." The rest of us didn't talk about it much. We were concentrating on ourselves, on surviving, on not becoming non-hackers.

During the third training week I was cleaning my boots outside the squad bay, perching them atop the water table of the huge and very old sinks out there. I was trying to direct the water along the edges of the boots, so as to force out every grain of dirt and dust in the seams, when a black hand came into my field of vision. The hand moved toward me and then rested upon mine, and for a moment I was so miserable about everything that I did not even look up right away to see whose hand it was. We didn't have many black people in the PLC program at that time, but I was so miserable and exhausted at that moment that I didn't care.

When I did look up, I saw a candidate there, not one from our company, K Company, but one from the next company down, L, or Lima Company. I had seen his face before, at drill or in the mess hall or on a physical training run. It was faces that you remembered in the military, faces without names.

The candidate grinned at me. There was something wrong here, I could tell. He had a strange look on his face. He grinned and pointed down at his feet. I looked. The feet were raw and red, wrapped in gauze, with pink fluid oozing along the wrap lines.

"Hill Trail," said the candidate. "Hill Trail did this to me," he said, and then he lifted his face to the sky, and he laughed, long and harsh. He laughed.

I went back to cleaning my boots. The other candidate moved

away. He was too strange. Had the Hill Trail made him that way?

I tried not to think about the Hill Trail. I was doing okay in the PLC classroom work, but the physical training was tough, and sometimes I wasn't sure I could make it. And we hadn't been tested yet. We hadn't been to the Hill Trail, but we knew it was coming.

The day before our Hill Trail exercise, we learned to make up and don the field marching pack—a complex, World War II–era, interlocking web of rucksacks and haversacks, laced together with weapon belts and suspenders, and a camouflaged field shelter half rolled tightly and fastened up and over the shoulders. I looked in the squad bay mirror as I assembled the pack, and I looked like something in pictures from the Civil War.

An M14 rifle with its wooden stock was belted over the right shoulder tightly so that it would rest parallel to the marching pack. I looked in the mirror again, and now I looked more like the marines who had landed on Tarawa or Saipan in World War II. Had we not come far since World War II?

We worked in pairs to get the packs right, because we knew we would be wearing them on the Hill Trail the next day. We assembled them, disassembled them, and tightened them, so that they wouldn't slide or bump or chafe the next day, and bring us down, or make parts of us end up like the feet of the Lima Company candidate. Our sergeant instructor, I think his name was John Holcombe, helped us. He never talked much. We knew he had just returned from a Vietnam tour, but we never learned much about him.

The field marching pack felt very heavy. I thought of the L Company candidate's feet, and I had a bad feeling about the next day.

Hill Trail day dawned soft and warm, ominous in that its

early-morning warmth portended high midday temperatures. I imagined the ancient Erinyes waiting for us out there, goddesses of death waiting to cut down candidates whose times had come. In morning formation I could feel the heat already, and I did not like it.

I had assumed we would skip the morning physical training because of the Hill Trail exercise that lay ahead, but I was wrong. So many common-sense ideas I had brought with me were wrong in this world.

Sergeant Holcombe led the physical training himself that morning, through the push-ups, sit-ups, and side-straddle hops, and even the formation run around the perimeter of Camp Upshur. I could already feel the sweat curling across my forehead as the sun was coming up. I definitely had a bad feeling about this day.

After morning chow, which I did not eat because I just couldn't, the platoon geared up in their field marching packs, and then we marched along the dirt-packed streets of the camp to the corrugated-steel armory where they gave us our M14s. They were very careful with those rifles. Mostly we conducted training at Camp Upshur without actual weapons. That was probably wise, considering the way some of the candidates felt about Staff Sergeant McNab.

Our sergeant instructors formed us up on the far side of the mess hall, Staff Sergeant McNab and Sergeant Holcombe stepped to the sides, and our officer appeared in front of us.

We never saw our officer much, 1st Lt. John J. Smith, our platoon commander. He too had just come back from a Vietnam tour, and he had a scar across the side of his face. We never saw him in any uniform but a field uniform, the utilities. One of the candidates whose father was a doctor said that the lieutenant smelled of alcohol sometimes in the morning, but I was never sure about that. He was tall and he seemed strong and tough, but he never talked much, and we never got much of an idea of what he was like.

Next to me in the formation, looking straight ahead but talking softly from the side of his mouth, was another candidate, someone named Brown. I remember it clearly, because I didn't want him whispering to me. I didn't want to be distracted in any way from what lay just ahead. I wanted to conserve and focus every bit of energy and concentration I had on what was coming, and what had to be done that day. But that was not how Brown did it.

"I have a bad feeling about this one today," he whispered. He was from Rhode Island, he talked funny—like he had marbles in his mouth—and I did not like him.

"I don't want to go," he said.

What he needed from me I could not give.

"Are you scared, David?" he asked.

I said nothing to him.

"Can we make it, David?" he asked.

All I felt for him was anger, anger emerging from the haze of fatigue, heat, sweat, fear, and ill-fitting, scratchy uniforms. Anger from six weeks in this godforsaken camp. Anger at this other candidate's need for something from me that I could not give that day. I felt this for the first time in my life, the anger that could turn to hurting.

I was trying to listen carefully to the lieutenant.

"We're going up the Hill Trail today, candidates," said Lieutenant Smith.

"Keep it tight, today, candidates," he said. "Keep it tight up against the man in front of you." I was wondering why.

"Face to the right," said Lieutenant Smith.

He said the words in a low-key way, not with the rancor of

almost everything Staff Sergeant McNab said. I wondered if the time in Vietnam, the time that had given him that scar on his face, had given him this flatness in the way he talked.

We faced to the right. There was precision in the movement. You could hear the sounds of boots on the gravel, a grinding, and the sound was ominous. My stomach spasmed.

Lieutenant Smith took his place at the front and right of the column.

"Forward march!" he said. Each candidate stepped his left foot forward; Sergeant Instructor Holcombe moved out to the left side, parallel to the column; and Staff Sergeant McNab took his place in the rear of the column, to be there for those who would be falling out. I determined that it would not be me.

The company swung out onto the gravel surface of what they called the Grinder, behind the training area, headed for the low Virginia hills just beyond. I said to myself, this is not so bad. This doesn't hurt. There is nothing here I can't do. There was a rhythm to the leather boots crunching the gravel, a rhythm that was firm and strong, and we were singing now, the chants of U.S. military training in the twentieth century.

We moved out past the Grinder and along the base of the ridgeline behind the training area, into a single long green column, four platoons moving together, with the flash suppressors of the M14 rifles sticking up alongside steel helmets, everything in order underneath the morning Virginia sun. For a while I thought this day would not be so bad.

Soon, to the left, we could see the opening in the trees where power lines swept up through the forests, almost straight up the rocky hillside to the ridgeline above, and then to another ridgeline that we could not see, and another, and another. But we didn't think of this or look up for long. We watched the boots of the candidate in front of us, and we tried to keep our strides tight behind him. Candidate Brown was in front of me, and I tried to place my boots just where he had stepped.

We swept up the rocky space along the power lines, and the pace seemed to quicken. Each step became heavier and tougher than the one before it. I bent forward. I shifted the field marching pack higher onto my back. In my mind's eye, I tried to get the weight of the pack to pull me forward instead of dragging me backward. K Company turned into the gaping yaw of the Hill Trail, and here everything became very hard.

We kept going uphill. I didn't understand how the steps could be stretching out longer as the inclination rose, but they did. The shouts of the sergeant instructor in front and the ominous growls of the platoon sergeant in back rose like ancient clarion calls of pain and violence. The field marching packs heaved and shifted, and any angles in the gear began to sear themselves into adjacent flesh. There was no stopping. And the pace was such that there was no space for even a pause to adjust a belt or tighten a hitch in the mounting of the pack. There was pain, and the question arose in my mind: would I be able to take it?

Dust began to rise, because it had been dry, and the boots of the candidates in front were churning and roiling the ground. My eyes watered. My feet began to slip some, and I knew I had to stop that backward sliding or effectively run each step of the Hill Trail twice, an impossible task. Candidate Brown was slipping even worse in front of me. I tried not to think of him as a person—just feet in front—watching him so if he fell he wouldn't bring me down. I had no thoughts of helping him.

An accordion effect began, spacing out and closing up that occurred if each man did not keep it tight against the man immediately in front of him. Candidate Brown and I were about halfway down the line, so the pitching and clumping of the accordion effect was less. For a brief moment I felt pity for those poor candidates in the rear of the column, where the accordion would be smashing and tearing at their souls before this day was over. I felt better then, because I knew that the others behind me were faring worse this day.

The company churned its way higher on the trail. I tried to concentrate all my thoughts and power on little things, where this boot went, where that rock was, where the backside of Candidate Brown was in front of me. I tried to keep my breathing steady and calm. No hyperventilation, I told myself. No panic. I tried to harden my thoughts. I summoned the anger that can emerge from pain and suffering, and I turned the anger onto the Hill Trail itself, my enemy this day.

Time seemed to drift and wander, up and down. The trail rose up and up in front of us, canteens clanked against cartridge belts, and rifles clanged against steel helmets. I couldn't tell how long we had been going. I was floating through the rhythm of the column. The dust rose. The sun climbed higher in the sky. I could hear Staff Sergeant McNab shouting and angry somewhere behind. Time passed and I wasn't aware of it. This was a good sign. I was making it.

The pain lessened. There was nothing for me now but the swinging rhythm of the hike, and the marines swinging their route ever higher, ever farther into the forest.

The rising heat of the Virginia summer was there now, in our faces as we moved along. I told myself, let the heat come. Let it meet my anger. Make it hotter. I was winning the fight this day. I was learning that this was how it felt to win.

In front of me, Candidate Brown's utility jacket was getting wetter and wetter with sweat—first around the edges and straps of his pack, then staining the jacket dark green. The sweat spread until the entire jacket was dark with moisture. Too much sweat. I knew he wasn't going to make it that day. I wanted to keep away from him.

And still we moved on. After a time we seemed to be moving laterally along the ridgelines, perhaps curving back to the south, high above Camp Upshur. Time became confusing. We kept going, and everything was jumbled up in my mind.

I felt stronger now, not weaker. Dusty, delirious, and angry, I felt surges of dark energy, and my boot strikes became sharper. I crashed into Brown when he slipped at one point, and I screamed at him to tighten it up.

Others were not making it. Some had dropped out. I had seen them lying in ditches beside the trail, seeming to flow back and past me as we swung along. I didn't look closely. I felt nothing for them. I had never been like this before. There was exhilaration to it.

Toward midday, perhaps after several hours, I let myself think briefly of the candidate whose bandaged feet I'd seen. I studied the impact of my boots in the red dirt; "9R," I thought. The 9R boots I was wearing fit perfectly. A small thing that could make the difference between hacking and non-hacking: the fit of one's boots. I wondered for a second if it was small things that made the difference across the Pacific in Vietnam where we were headed. Small things like— Well, I didn't know what. I shut off these wandering thoughts and focused on the trail. I felt no pain. I felt I could keep doing this forever.

The sun burned higher in the sky. Staff Sergeant McNab came jangling and clamoring up along the left side of the column—

accelerating past the rest of us with physical strength and endurance that must have come from a lifetime of physical hardening in the Corps. He was shouting to us as he passed—shouting words to us as if he had looked inside our souls, understood our pain, and was talking to it.

"See that pine tree on the next ridgeline?" he yelled. Up and down the green line, over and over, he screamed, "See that pine tree?"

I looked. Everything was moving up and down. There were many pine trees.

"We will stop to rest when we get to that pine tree, candidates!" shouted Staff Sergeant McNab. He stopped toward the front, and he screamed at us as we passed him. "Hang in there!" he shouted. "Rest is coming at that tree!"

Many looked up for that pine tree as if it were the Holy Grail, and we the wandering Knights Templar. I felt I could see it, too. That must be the tree, I thought, at the top of the next ridgeline, not that far. The thought of rest changed me. I felt that I needed to stop, needed to rest now. Staff Sergeant McNab was being merciful to us, and now I changed over—I desperately wanted that mercy. His harsh qualities seemed to dissolve in my mind, his image became suffused with warmth and kindness, and I felt gratitude. I felt for this strange moment that I loved Staff Sergeant McNab; it was a profound and deep sense of love. Things would be all right now, I could feel it. This man, Staff Sergeant McNab, was going to let us rest.

Now I bowed my head down with relief. The rocks passed by with every step beneath me, and I loved those rocks; even the dust that rose about us was more pleasant because we were going to rest when we reached that pine tree.

Then a terrible thing happened, something terrible beyond

anything I had ever known or imagined, unspeakable in its pain: we reached the pine tree, it was there in front of us, and we did not stop. We did not even slow. We just kept going, and the tree moved past us, disappearing behind us in the dust.

For the first time, cries rang out from the candidates, cries of pain, anger, and protest. I had never heard these cries before, nor had I expected ever to hear them. And from the rear came the growling voice of "Pleasant Moments" McNab.

"You wanted to stop, didn't you!!" he screamed now, and the scream was harsh and angry. It carried forward up and down the column, and his voice brought despair to our hearts.

"Well, we're not stopping!" Staff Sergeant McNab screamed again. "Take the pain!" he bellowed. "Are you weak? Are you non-hackers? You candidates don't deserve a rest!" And on he went. "You're weak," he said, and now his voice was dropping, gravelly and sadistic. "Do you think the gooners will stop when you're tired?" A lifetime of hating and killing Asians was in his voice. "Well, they won't!" he screamed. "They won't and I won't and you won't!" He continued, but I was no longer listening, just putting one boot in front of the other until—until what, I didn't know.

I can't recall much of what happened on the Hill Trail hike after we passed by the pine tree. Later there were fragments of memories: shouting and heat waves shimmering, flashing scenes of trees and the trail—candidates falling, the sergeant instructor yelling. It turned out, I think, that we were closer to Camp Upshur after the pine tree than any of us knew—we were near the end of the exercise. The trail turned down after that into the camp, and we could see it, those of us who could still look up. There was an open grassy field outside the camp and when we came to that field, I remember, they had a candidate bugler standing on one of the platforms in the obstacle course blowing the staccato notes of the cavalry charge. Then everything broke down, everyone was running and falling, and the bugler continued.

There we were, back in the camp, ragged and broken up, trying to get the remnants of the company lined up for roll call outside the squad bay, picturing cool water, our bunk, and rest, but everything was messed up. I remember pushing some of the candidates, getting them to stand in formation so we could see who was there and who was not, because I knew we had straggled out there on the trail, and for the first time I began to think that I should worry about that—about finding them and organizing the survivors. I remember looking down the line of the formation in the shimmering heat and seeing men wander and waver and fall, some forward, some backward, some without even trying to protect themselves. Ambulances were there. And it occurred to me—I could feel it—that things were really out of control, and that the exercise wasn't supposed to be this way. I was screaming, I remember that. I was moving candidates inside, out of the heat, screaming at them, grabbing them, and dragging some of them inside. Sergeant Holcombe had the primitive camp showers streaming, and I was dragging fallen candidates into the cold water. I remember the bodies lying on the sun-baked gravel outside, and me moving them inside, yelling, screaming, and ordering others to move them inside where it was dark and cool.

Later, very gradually, things softened, quieted down, and the soaked green company of marine officer candidates sat quietly, cool showers washed down upon all, and things were better.

I left the showers and walked down the center aisle of the squad bay to the swinging screen doors. Outside was the hot Virginia sun. I opened a door and stepped outside, and I watched jeeps and ambulances bringing down stragglers and heat-injured candidates from the hillside. In the back of one jeep, lying on his side and very still, was Candidate Brown. I had already seen enough that day to know that he was dead. I turned and went back inside the squad bay, where order was being restored, cool water was being drunk by everyone, and the sergeant instructor was helping candidates still drenched from the cold showers to strip off their field marching packs and lie down in their bunks. There was a large pedestal fan at one end of the squad bay, and the sergeant instructor got this fan going so that it filled the entire bay with moving air. And we rested.

At the end of this day, after the sun had moved low in the sky and the company had had chow and was resting again in its bunks, Staff Sergeant McNab came into the squad bay, and he placed his hand on my shoulder. It was the first time he had touched me—and it was with that deformed hand from the road to Koto Ri.

"You did good today, Candidate Nelson," said the staff sergeant. "You took charge today," he said, and then he turned and left.

Later that night, while others were in the sleep of exhaustion, I lay awake in my bunk. The droning of the pedestal fan continued, massaging the warm night air of the Old South. The gray, half-turned visage of Candidate Brown's broken form was in my mind, and I knew it would never leave me, that it would be there till my last day. I wondered how many other young men had passed through the gravel streets of Camp Upshur to their deaths in Asian wars, beginning with Guadalcanal in 1942.

I thought of Lee Roy. I wondered how he was doing in the Mainside camp where the PLC seniors were. Lee Roy would be finishing soon, and then he would go home. I wished that I could see him sooner so I could tell him what had happened at Camp

Upshur. I lay awake, and I thought of what Staff Sergeant Mc-Nab had said. I was changing. I could feel it, the change inside me, from today and from many other things that had happened here in this dusty and forlorn camp. I could feel myself hardening inside—putting things there that had not been there before and would never fully go away. I reached up and slid my fingers along the scabbard of the bayonet that hung from the iron rail of the bunk above.

The remaining four weeks of the PLC combined course were less eventful. It was as if the Hill Trail experience had served as a cauldron for us all, candidates and staff, hardening us, forging us together in the bonds of shared experience, and that everything that had been before the Hill Trail was in a different world. The training continued—map reading, tactics, Marine Corps history, physical fitness, weapons, and drill, drill, drill. But the end was coming now. Those left were going to graduate. And we would be going home.

In the second week before the end of the camp, at mail call on Tuesday, I received a letter from Lee Roy. The letter had a Lubbock postmark, but Lee Roy had written on USMC stationery that he must have bought at Mainside, and in the faint watermark behind the ink-scrawled address were the four marines raising the flag at the top of Mount Suribachi on Iwo Jima. It was addressed to Lance Corporal David L. Nelson, 2217344, Marine Corps Base, Quantico, Virginia. I guessed that was me now, Lance Corporal David L. Nelson, 2217344. I have to admit that I kind of liked it, the way that letter was addressed.

"Among many other things, which will have to wait until you return," wrote Lee Roy, "I have to tell you that I was the 'Honor Man' for my company down at Mainside! Can you believe it?"

David Nelson has his M14 ready for action on the banks of the Potomac River during officer candidate training in the summer of 1966. The photo was sent to his hometown newspaper, the *Lubbock Avalanche-Journal*, which published it on August 24, 1966. Official U.S. Marine Corps photo.

I pondered it all. I let the letter slide down against my shorts while I sat on the edge of my bunk. Yes, I thought. I could believe it. I had survived but Lee Roy had been the honor man.

I could hear Lee Roy gung ho-ing around every person in Lubbock who would listen, and I smiled to myself. That would be Lee Roy, all right. The lights went out in the squad bay, and I folded the letter into the top drawer of my green, wooden sea chest at the foot of the bunk.

And then the final day came. The ten weeks of the PLC senior course were ending. Those who were left had made it.

There was a parade. Not much of a parade, one had to concede. A small parade on the Grinder. A few families who lived locally came and sat in aged green stands, and in those families were a few teenage girls—the most beautiful girls I thought that I had ever seen, even though I couldn't see them well from where

I was. We were allowed to wear the khaki undress uniform of the Marine Corps for the parade, instead of the tan shirt and green pants combination, which had been our imago as candidates during our time in the camp. The company was allowed to have a flag, four of us were chosen as color bearers, and I was chosen to carry the rifle on the starboard flank. That was something. I looked at myself in a mirror before we walked out. The clean uniform fit tightly, and the green cartridge belt was snug around my waist. I looked like a marine. Would I become one? Was I already? I looked in the mirror. Outside, buses were waiting, buses that would take us home. And what would happen after that? How would I—how would all of us—be different? Was I really going to do this? Would I be back for The Basic School next year? There was so much changing; there were so many questions. I walked outside the squad bay with my fellows from Kilo Company for the last time.

[6]
1967
There Is a War Yonder

"How did you do it, Lee Roy? The honor man part, I mean, down there at Quantico?"

Lee Roy and I sat talking again on the bleachers by the playa lake, and we watched the colors of the West Texas sunset. It was August 1966, and our senior year at Texas Tech would begin the next week. Our time in Lubbock would be over after that, and our conversations by the lake would end too. I think we both knew that, without actually saying it.

"There are some hard things in the Marine Corps, Davey," he said. "It's not like out here," and he swept his hand across the panorama.

Lee Roy was reflecting on it all, as was I.

"And you've just got to do those hard things, Davey," he said. "That's what the oath means."

Lee Roy had just finished beating me on the tennis court. It all came so natural to him, the strength, the quickness, and the winning.

He turned his head to look at me.

"You did it, too," he said.

"I made it, Lee Roy, but I wasn't the honor man," I said. I spoke softly. I was not Lee Roy. I tended to speak more quietly than he did about important things. "There's a big difference."

"How big, Davey?" he asked. He was still looking at me. "Charles Lance couldn't make it because of his old leg injury. That makes me, you, and maybe one other guy from all of Texas Tech, all classes. That's not that many when you consider the country is at war."

Lee Roy felt bitterness about the politics of some students at Tech.

"Yeah, well you were there, Davey. You were there," he said.

Lee Roy could say things and make a person believe that things were right, that things would turn out well, and that evil would not triumph in the world. Lee Roy had that ability.

"I was mainly there because—," I was trying to get this right, "because of you, Lee Roy," I said.

Praise was hard for him to accept and even acknowledge. He just nodded a little.

"Are you going to do it, Lee Roy?" I asked.

"Do what?" He turned to me again. He didn't see it the way I saw it, that now there was a big decision in front of us.

"The marines, Lee Roy. We'll be seniors at Tech, now. We'll have to decide next year. Are you really going to do it? Go in?"

"What else would I do?" he asked. That was the way it was for Lee Roy. Our troops were fighting in Vietnam, and for Lee Roy there wasn't even a decision.

For me, there was more to it. The news from Vietnam was casualties every day. The 3rd Marine Division had moved up to the demilitarized zone in Quang Tri Province, and the 1st Marines had come from California and landed in the flat country and river valleys west of Da Nang. Walter Cronkite reported on the shooting and the bombing daily on the *CBS Evening News*.

"Well, Lee Roy," I said, quietly, "you know it's one thing to do the PLC training. We all learned a lot from that. It helped us grow up. But we don't have to really go, you know," I said. I could tell it had sounded wrong to Lee Roy as soon as the words were out.

"The country needs us, David," he said.

That was all there was to it. The country needed us.

"Well, Lee Roy," I carried on, but changing direction a little here. "Did you see the letter about the PLC law program last week?" We had all gotten the letter. This was a program in which you could get a second lieutenant commission at graduation from college, but instead of reporting directly to The Basic School at Quantico, you could be deferred for three years while attending law school. After that you would have to attend The Basic School but then you would be posted to the Fleet as a lawyer, not as an infantry officer.

"You know, Lee Roy, I was thinking about that letter—about maybe being a lawyer, someday. You know I started out as a pre-law major at Tech."

Lee Roy said nothing. He looked back out at the playa lake and the sunset.

A month later I signed up to take the Law School Aptitude Test.

The fall of 1966 moved along. The news from Vietnam continued to be bad. We heard about big battles in places like Pleiku and Con Thien, and now there were Medal of Honor stories, many of them. Lee Roy reveled in these, but they made me uncomfortable. I remember something Staff Sergeant McNab had said: "We don't want any Medal of Honor winners from this platoon, when your time comes to go over there. The Medal of Honor is a losing medal!" I recall just how he said it, emphasizing the word "losing" so strongly that it jolted us. "When you get over, make sure the medals all go to the gooners!" His eyes lit up. "Make sure they're all gook Medals of Honor over there!" That was the only time I had heard him say "gook" instead of "gooner." As best I could tell, that was Staff Sergeant McNab's way of designating a Vietnamese person, as opposed to "gooners" from other Asian countries.

I came to realize that Staff Sergeant McNab would be with me from here on, making comments and reminding me forever of his gravelly philosophy of life.

The end of the year approached, and we had Christmas with our families in Lubbock, as always. For one last time, everything was the same. We knew 1967 would bring change.

On February 3, Lee Roy, Charles Lance, and I brought dates to Mackenzie Park, in the ancient river valley on the east side of Lubbock. We roasted wieners and marshmallows, and it was pretty much a disaster as a date, because it was so cold that all we could do was try to keep our hands near the fire to warm them a little. The hot dogs wouldn't even cook. Winter in West Texas can be like that. I think the coldest I have ever been was out in winter winds coming off the llanos.

I don't remember the girls who were our dates that night, not one of them. But I remember the month and day because something was changing about the way we were with girls. That I could tell.

Lee Roy's date called him Lee. I had not heard that before, and I wondered what it meant. I didn't say anything, but I wondered if he was altering his name a little, getting ready for the end of his time in West Texas later that spring. It was like he was going to be a new person when he left for Quantico and The Basic School later that summer, the summer of 1967, and he would need a new name to go with it, one that was more East Coast than Lee Roy, which kind of marks you as a Texan or at least a southerner. I'm sure something like that was happening.

Although I can't remember who my date was that night, I remember thinking that I would like someone I could get to know, could see again, something like that. This was new for me. Before, dates with girls had been just things to do at certain times during the school year. Now I was feeling something different. I don't know where that came from, especially since things would be so unstable for all of us, with graduation coming and all. I wondered if Lee Roy was feeling something like this too.

While we were trying to melt the marshmallows and heat the hot dogs, I thought of a letter that my aunt in Temple, Texas, had written to me, and which had arrived that day. She had written me to say that I should look up Martie Lowry, who was also a senior at Tech. Martie's parents were my aunt and uncle's friends, and they all thought that Martie and I might be a good fit. There I was sitting by a windblown fire in Mackenzie Park with one girl, and I was thinking about this letter on my desk at home about another.

Charles Lance didn't say much that night, as I recall. He had been forced to drop out of the PLC program the previous summer, because of a pin he had in one of his legs, from an operation to repair a fracture suffered during a fishing trip. Lee Roy had probably saved his life on that fishing trip, after Charles had fallen and broken his leg, but we didn't talk about those things now. Our discussions were about the things ahead. We didn't exactly say it, but we could feel that the time of our youth in West Texas was about to be left behind.

On February 6 the Southern Methodist University (SMU) School of Law notified me that I had been awarded a full-tuition scholarship. The amount was $1,350—$675 for each semester—which at that time was a lot of money, enough to make the difference between my being able to go or not. My grandfather had always wanted to attend SMU, he had told me, but he could never afford to go there. SMU was in Dallas, and to many people growing up in Lubbock it meant a lot to be able to go to the big city. I said yes.

On February 14 I applied to the Marine Corps for a transfer to PLC-Law, and on March 2 they notified me of my acceptance. I would not go into the infantry. I would not go to war. I was going to law school.

On February 10 I had my first date with Martie Lowry. She had soft brown hair and soft brown eyes. She even spoke softly, and not a lot—kind of like me. She knew my family from the Temple area and was even prettier than my aunt had said. She was an education major at Texas Tech, and wanted to teach when she was done. I liked that. Over the next three months Martie and I had forty-eight dates. I counted them, wrote them down—I was always something of an accountant. Martie and I didn't talk a lot when we were together. We didn't have to, we just kind of fit. It gradually dawned on us that we were always together, and we wanted to always be together. I don't remember a time when I asked her to marry me. It became something we both knew we were going to do.

You could say that Martie and I were meant for each other, and maybe there was a higher power involved in our meeting. People say those things, but I don't know. There was something about the times—1967. It was the year of the big battles in Vietnam, or so we thought, because we didn't know that 1968 would be even worse, and 1969 bigger yet. We heard constantly on radio and television about fights along the demilitarized zone—the DMZ. The marines were fighting at the Rockpile and in Quang Tri Province and other places with strange nicknames. I always thought they should have called that area "the militarized zone" because so much fighting seemed to be going on there. I tried to make a joke about that once to Lee Roy, but things seemed less funny when 1967 came around. Lee Roy and I were finishing college, we were in the PLC program, and events seemed to be moving too fast. Like an accountant, I wanted to write things down, measure them and count them as they came by, but nothing could stop or even slow what was happening.

I think Lee Roy was affected by all of this too. He didn't say anything to me about it, but I think he was feeling the same things I was feeling.

I didn't tell Lee Roy about law school right away. It came out because Cecil Puryear got married in March, and Lee Roy, Charles Lance, and I all attended the wedding. Afterward we drove around for a while, then ended up in Charles's driveway. We talked about things, I remember. We weren't drinking beer. We just sat in the car and talked.

I told Lee Roy and Charles that I might become a marine JAG officer. I had already signed up for the PLC-Law program, but the way I put it that night was more tentative. I wanted to know how Lee Roy saw it, whether he would approve.

It was dark, so I couldn't see his facial expressions, but I had the feeling that Lee Roy was disappointed in me, disappointed because I'd chosen law over the infantry. I still have that feeling today.

Lee Roy himself would be going soon. That was clear to the three of us, sitting in a car in Charles Lance's driveway in March

1967. It had started with our going off to PLC camps the previous year, but now it would just be Lee Roy going. As big a step as those camps were, it was bigger to actually do it—to head off for The Basic School at Quantico, and after that to "WestPac." The Western Pacific was what they referred to in those days. The three of us all knew Lee Roy had a big step ahead. I think that's why we talked for so long, even though we didn't address the war. I felt bad afterward that we hadn't talked about it. But we were young, and it was hard to find the words.

On April 28, the Semper Fi Society at Texas Tech had a party at Reese Air Force Base, out on the west side of town where the long strips of asphalt lay that glider pilots had used in 1943 to train for Normandy. Marine Corps recruiters from Lubbock attended, and officer selection officers (OSOs) came from Dallas. Lee Roy and Charles came with their dates, and I brought Martie. It wasn't much of a party, I suppose, by Houston or Dallas standards, amidst white clapboard walls and concrete floors. We had put up some U.S. flags and some red and yellow USMC flags, punch and cookies were served on a long table with folding legs, some of the younger Tech students who had signed up for PLC came, and all of us were dressed up. The recruiters and the OSOs wore their uniforms, of course.

I introduced Martie to Lee Roy and Charles, and I told Lee Roy and Charles that I was going to the SMU School of Law, and not The Basic School. We didn't have our uniforms then, since we would not be commissioned until graduation day. We wore the thin ties and ribbed cotton sport coats of the mid-sixties, and our dates wore dresses that had some frills that made them blossom a little.

Lee Roy didn't seem to say much. He appeared to be deep in thought that night.

On May 25, Martie and I went to Zales on Broadway in Lubbock. I had saved $220 from my part-time job in the warehouse at the Ben E. Keith Company, where my father worked, and we got an engagement ring for Martie, as well as two gold wedding rings, for that price. It was a good deal. I still wear the ring we bought that day.

June 3 was graduation from Tech. Martie was graduating too. I remember that we stood in line outside the Lubbock Municipal Coliseum, where the ceremony was to be held. Lee Roy was there. I reintroduced him to Martie—he didn't seem to remember her. There were so many people, and everyone was talking. Parents were there. We had to keep moving. Inside the diplomas were waiting for us. It was too much for me to make sense of it all. But I recall that Lee Roy didn't seem to remember Martie. I told him that we were going to get married, and he was polite but I couldn't tell what it meant to him. There was a lot going on.

Martie and I got married on August 28. Martie Sue Lowry had been her name before the ceremony, and afterward it became Martie Lowry Nelson. That always seemed momentous to me, that changing of a person's name.

We had a candlelight ceremony at First Methodist Church in Temple. Since we weren't married in Lubbock, I think it was this night that really made me feel that I was leaving—leaving my childhood, my family, and my growing-up place, the home I would always be from whenever people should ask.

We had a reception in the church, and then Martie and I had to leave that evening to return to Irving, because I had to show up to start law school the next day. Around Waco we stopped to get something to eat in a Texaco truck stop, as I remember. We sat there and ate hamburgers, people looked at us, and I wonder

In his dress whites soon after a June 7, 1967, commissioning ceremony, Lee Roy Herron holds his Marine Corps cover while wearing fresh white gloves. Courtesy of the Herron family.

In a freeze frame from a 16mm film of a June 7, 1967, ceremony, Lee Roy Herron (left) and David Nelson (center) are sworn in as U.S. Marine Corps officers. Their second lieutenant gold bars were pinned on immediately following the event. Courtesy of Norval "Tex" Thomas.

if they could tell that we had just been married. Looking back on it now, I feel bad that everything was so rushed. There was no time—and there was no money.

By then Lee Roy had left too. He had to report to The Basic School on or about August 28, because they started a new class on the first day of each month back then, and they wanted new officers to report a day or two beforehand. Usually the young lieutenants started on July 1 or August 1, but for some reason they postponed Lee Roy until September.

So Lee Roy didn't come to our wedding. But from what I heard later from him, I think that Martie's and my relationship and marriage had affected him. Lee Roy was changing some things too that summer.

July 1, 1967
Lubbock, Texas

Lee Roy Herron sat near the telephone in his parents' home, on the sofa, near the end table. He looked down at the phone. It was one of those new colored plastic ones, with a circle of numbers in the center. Lee Roy stared at the phone, hesitating.

After a time he reached across with his right hand and dialed seven numbers.

"Hello, Danelle," he said. "Danny," he quickly corrected it. "Danny, yes," he said.

"You may not remember me," said Lee Roy. There was a pause. "Oh, well, yes," he said.

"I saw your sister Sherryl today, downtown by the park," said Lee Roy. "She said I might— She said it might be okay if I called." He closed his eyes. He listened.

"Yes," he said.

"I heard you were home from college this summer," said Lee Roy.

Danelle had not gone to Texas Tech like the rest of us. She was a year behind us in school and had gone to LIFE Bible College in Los Angeles. This was a school that brought the Bible into college education in a serious way.

"Do you think it might be all right if," and here it was hard for Lee Roy, "if I could see you?"

It wasn't that Lee Roy had not dated girls before. He had, and he had always seemed fairly comfortable with it all. But this time it was different. He was calling up Danelle Davis because she had been in his mind the whole time, I think, from the cheerleading days in junior high. Older people can say what they want about these things that happen in school gymnasiums and locker rooms, but I say that most of us remember names and faces from this time in our lives. And I believe Lee Roy felt strongly about Danelle, saw what Martie and I were doing, and was experiencing the same feelings. Maybe he was looking for something to hold on to in a world that was in motion. In 1967, young men in America needed something to hold on to, whichever way things went.

Danelle was the daughter of Bennie and Doc Davis, and she had one sister, Sherryl. All of them had a kind of sunshine in their manner, even though they never had much money. Nobody in Lubbock had much money in those years. The Davises had been named Lubbock Family of the Year in 1958, and that was saying something about their character—the way they were, the way people felt about them.

The other thing about the Davis family, and about Danelle in particular, that was having an impact on Lee Roy was their religion. When we were growing up in Lubbock, Lee Roy's family went to one of the Methodist churches off University Avenue, in the northeast part of the city. But the way the Davises did religion was seriously beyond that, and there was something about this that felt right to Lee Roy in 1967. Something about the stability and the solidity of it. I think that Lee Roy saw something in that family that he was missing and wanting at that time, because afterward he became a true believer in a way that he never had before. The times were changing, and Lee Roy was changing with them.

[7]

1967

And a Man Shall Leave His Mother

October 1967

Marine Corps Base, Quantico

Camp Barrett, O'Bannon Hall

The Basic School

There are pictures on the east wall of the entrance foyer at The Basic School, Camp Barrett, Quantico. Young marine officers train at Camp Barrett before they go to the Fleet, and they see the pictures there of young men, tense and stiff in close-buttoned uniform, decades dead.

Under the photos are terse accounts of deeds and death, clumsy words from people more used to fighting than writing: "Conspicuous gallantry, above and beyond the call of duty."

And above each citation, medals—curling, sky-blue ribbons, each with thirteen white stars. The Medal of Honor wall at The Basic School, each face a hero.

"Refusing evacuation although mortally wounded . . ."

All of them had been lieutenants, just like the young men passing through the Camp Barrett entrance and looking at their faces. "There have been others before you," the grim-faced pictures seem to say, "and there will be others after you."

"Single-handedly attacking the machine gun emplacement . . ."

In their faces the foreboding of what lay ahead, even then, before they went across the Pacific, before they left The Basic School. They too had once walked the halls of Camp Barrett. Rows and rows of faces and citations on a wall, and in the faces death, and near the close of most of those citations these words: "He gallantly gave his life for his country."

Covered with the red dirt of the Virginia hills, the soil caked along the edges of his boots and in the seams of his utility uniform, 2nd Lt. Lee Roy Herron stood looking at the faces on the wall. It was October now. Lieutenant Herron held his M14 at its balance point in his right hand, took off his steel helmet with his left hand, and looked into the faces.

"We've got a poem for you, Lee," came a chorus of strong voices from behind him. Lee Roy whirled around, the muzzle of the M14 cutting a long circular path through the air.

Three other Basic School second lieutenants stood behind Lee Roy, dressed like he was in the sateen green utility uniform of those days. They had their arms around each other's shoulders, and the center one held a field message note in his hand.

"Here's the poem, Lee." He smiled, snickered, and the other two bent forward and groaned as if they knew what was coming and that it would be painful.

"And the captain bold of Company B," read the center lieutenant, holding the page at a distance, as if it were a proclamation to some vast audience standing in front of him. One of the other two interrupted.

"That's you, Lee," he said, and they all laughed, and the reading had to begin again.

And the captain bold of Company B
Was a-fightin' in the lead,
Just like a true-born soldier he,
Of them bullets took no heed.

It was over, but all three laughed so hard that the paper drifted down to the tile floor, and the three held onto each other to keep from falling.

Lee Roy reached out to grab one of them around the neck, and then the other two wrapped their arms around Lee Roy, and then they were all laughing together, shaking and laughing and scattering red dirt and mud in the foyer of O'Bannon Hall.

This was Basic Class 1-68. Classes started each month, and were numbered according to their starting date within the U.S. government fiscal year, which begins September 1. Lee Roy's class started September 1, 1967, and therefore was numbered 1-68. That's the way the federal government does it.

There were many strange and cumbersome ways in the new world of the Marine Corps, things for the young lieutenants to learn: heads and bulkheads instead of bathrooms and walls, alphas and deltas instead of As and Ds, niners instead of nines, covers instead of hats. And after five months, at the end of January 1968, they would graduate from The Basic School, and no one needed to tell them where they would be going. The war in Vietnam was moving toward the climax of the big battles of 1968. Mostly the lieutenants did not talk about this except in a mechanical way, like noting where the 1st Marine Division was or who commanded the regiments of the 3rd.

Smiling now, Lee Roy and the others ambled down the windowed hallway, awkward with the weight and clumsiness of the

gear and guns they always carried, tools of death. Looking outside, Lee Roy could see the corrugated buildings of Camp Barrett,
among them the recycled uniform store, providing inexpensive,
never-used uniforms from previous Basic School attendees who
had left them there on contingency and now would never need
them. The tales of these young men were told around the camp.
Lee Roy listened to these war stories, and he was sure that he
was ready.

Later that evening, after the hundred second lieutenants of Basic Class 1-68 had finished dinner in the officers' mess on the
first floor of O'Bannon Hall, they sat in their two-person rooms,
wearing shorts and T-shirts, cleaning gear from the day's field ex-
ercises, talking and brushing, sitting cross-legged on their bunks.
Lee Roy sat intent upon the receiver of the M14 rifle on his lap,
a steel structure of many edges and angles, hard to reach with
a cloth or cotton swab. Lee Roy worked at it, wiping the small
grooves where the bolt would slide after a bullet fired. His roommate sat in the upper bunk, also cleaning a disassembled M14.
He was a short, muscular man with a strong New England accent and sometimes Lee Roy had trouble understanding him. The
bunks swayed a little, rhythmically, as they worked at the receiv-
ers of the rifles.

"We only have nine weeks left, Lee," said his bunkmate. "Nine
weeks until we graduate. What are you gonna do? I mean, what
are you going to decide? What MOS?"

Military occupational specialty: MOS. Every marine officer
had a primary MOS, and some of them had a secondary.

Lee Roy paused, and then he picked up the oiled rag he was
using and slid the thin film of oil across the steel once again.

"Do you know, Lee, my father was in the 1st Marine Division

in World War II? He was in the Guadalcanal landings. Do you know what he told me about that day—the day they landed?"

Lee Roy did not answer. He looked up again from his work on the M14, but he looked out the window of their room. Outside it was dark. For a moment, Lee Roy felt a wave of fear. He turned back to his M14.

"Well," continued the bunkmate above, "my father says they had them all lined up on the deck of the LST, the landing ship, tank, and they were going to have to go over those rope nets, you know, like we did last week down at the Little Creek exercise—same thing." The steel bunk was shaking to and fro with the bunkmate's polishing.

"Well," he continued, "they told the marines there, my father and the others, that 'some of you are going to get hurt on that island, and when you do, try to protect your 782 gear and your rifles because we can't replace those right now.'" The bunkmate polished some more. "That's what they told them," he said, and he was done.

After a time, Lee Roy set his cleaning gear down. He threaded the steel locking wire through the receiver of the M14 and clicked it around the frame of the lower bunk.

"I'm going downstairs to make a phone call from the Hawkins Room," said Lee Roy. He stood up in his white shorts and T-shirt. He wore the era's synthetic rubber sandals on his feet. All the lieutenants dressed like this in their bunk rooms.

"Well, you better put on your utility shirt or the student officer of the day will write you up," said the bunkmate.

"I'm not going to bother," said Lee Roy. He stood up, so that his head was now on the level of his bunkmate. The bunkmate looked at Lee Roy. He saw a crew-cut young man, plastic-frame glasses, blue eyes peering out carefully, dog tags jangling around his neck as always. The muscles of Lee Roy's chest were sharply defined, and he held himself erect, almost at attention.

Lee Roy walked out into the bright hallway of concrete-block walls and polished tile floors, then past open doors of lieutenant pairs sitting the same way, one high and one low, all of them cleaning and polishing shoes, boots, and rifles. A strong smell of cleaning oils, Kiwi polish, and Hoppe's No. 9 solution followed him down the hall. There was nothing on the walls and nothing to distinguish one room or pair of lieutenants from the next, except numbers on doors. Thanksgiving would be coming in a few weeks, but there were no decorations of any sort in the hallway or in the rooms. There were no holidays at Camp Barrett. There were no holidays in the Marine Corps, Lee Roy thought. He reached the end of the hall, and then went down steel steps to the level below.

Downstairs, near the snack room they called the Slop Chute, was the dimly lit Hawkins Room, a beer-only bar with pay telephones in booths along one wall. Here there was a photo of the burn-scarred face of 1st Lt. William D. Hawkins, killed leading his Scout Sniper Platoon from Japanese position to Japanese position along the dock at the Tarawa Atoll in 1943. When Hawkins had left home for the Pacific, he had told his family, "When I see you next it will be in heaven or in hell." And so it was.

Tonight Lee Roy went directly to the phones, dialing the operator for help with a long-distance call, asking for the area code for Los Angeles and then for the number for Danelle Davis's dormitory at LIFE College, and finally asking to make a collect, person-to-person call for her. On the other end, a young woman's voice answered, audible despite a crackling on the line. "Yes," the voice said, "I'll get her." There was some scrambling and scratching, and then Lee Roy heard another faint female voice, that of

Danelle Davis almost whispering to him on the other side of the continent. Lee Roy thought to himself that her voice was the sweetest thing he had ever heard.

"Yes," she said. "I'll accept the charges."

The operator left the line, and Lee Roy could speak directly with Danelle. His heart began to beat faster. He had rehearsed what he would say.

"Hello, Danny," he said. "How are you?"

He listened for a time.

"Well," said Lee Roy, "I guess I can't really say, but I just got it in my mind to call you tonight."

He listened again. He looked around, the receiver at his ear; the few other officers in the Hawkins Room were busy with other things.

Lee Roy gripped the receiver as tight as he did the receiver of his M14. "Well, that's what I was calling about," he said.

Lee Roy liked Danelle's voice. It had a rhythmic quality to it, a humming feeling and a softness. There was something soft and clear about her, something that made him feel that things in the world were indeed in order, just as Lee Roy said they were.

"Well," he said, "I know this may sound, well, it may sound too much—you may have other plans—you may not want to do it." Lee Roy paused again. "But Thanksgiving is coming, and I have some days off at Thanksgiving, what they call 'leave' in the Marine Corps," said Lee Roy.

He listened briefly, closed his eyes.

"Yes!" said Lee Roy. "That's what I was thinking." He opened his eyes, smiled.

"Are you sure it's not too much?" he asked. He listened again.

"The way things are here, I can't actually leave till Thanksgiving Day itself." He closed his eyes again. He nodded slightly. "Yes," he said. "I can't actually get there until the evening of Thanksgiving Day. Yes. Yes."

He listened, opened his eyes, smiled again. "I'll get the airplane ticket, Danny. I'll see you on Thanksgiving."

He'd done it.

October 1967

Irving, Texas

The Brentwood Apartments

After Martie and I got married, we moved into a one-bedroom apartment at the Brentwood Apartments, on South Nursery Road in Irving, Texas. These apartments were close to Bowie Junior High School, where Martie had gotten a job, so we thought she could walk to work, and we could save the gasoline cost of two commutes, since I had to drive back and forth to law school in Dallas. You had to live in the school district in which you taught, so we thought we might as well live close to the school.

I had exactly $400 left from my summer jobs, but I had it figured out that we could make it, at least through the first year. The apartment would cost us $115 per month, but it was completely furnished, and the utilities were included. Martie would make about $300 per month as a teacher. I figured with some luck, as long as we didn't buy any new clothes, we could make it.

I was driving a 1960 Ford Falcon those days. Martie had a car that her parents had given her before she had graduated from Temple High School—a 1962 Chevy II, white on the outside, with a red interior. She could drive that when she had to do errands or to school when the weather was bad. We ended up keeping that car for four more years. When I was assigned to Camp Lejeune, North Carolina, after I finished The Basic School,

I sold it to another marine for $125 just before I shipped overseas to Okinawa.

November 1967
MOS Day

The Basic School

With about six weeks to go before Basic Class 1-68 graduated, Military Occupational Specialty Day—MOS Day—came. At last the young lieutenants would choose the specialties they wanted.

In the reception area off the foyer of O'Bannon Hall, MOS stations had been set up. Mostly they were plain white tables, some with a few pictures on them, and an older officer from that specialty standing by to encourage, advertise his MOS, and hope to recruit the best members of Basic Class 1-68 into his field. In 1967 at Quantico, the older officer was typically some guy who was one or two Basic School cycles ahead of you, usually someone who had done his overseas tour and made it back.

Each Marine Corps MOS had a number. Infantry was 0300, artillery was 0800, and motor transport was 3500, among many others.

The second lieutenants of Basic Class 1-68 walked the hallway dressed up in their winter service green uniforms, black shoes, green gabardine trousers and blouses, khaki ties, and khaki shirts. Lee Roy thought it was the best uniform. He glanced at himself briefly as he passed the full-length mirror at the end of the hall, and liked what he saw.

"Motor T, Lee," came a voice from behind. Lee Roy did not need to look back. It was one of the authors of the doggerel about "the captain bold of Company B."

"Motor T and out in three, Lee," said the voice. "Stay alive with Thirty-five. Have you heard those sayings, Lee?"

"I'm infantry, George," said Lee Roy, still walking, not looking behind.

"Have you called the motor pool lately, Lee?" Another poet's voice. "We got two byes, four byes, six byes, and those big muthas that go AWHOOOSH!" Lee Roy again did not bother to look around.

"Infantry is where it's at," said Lee Roy, striding straight ahead. "No hiding and sliding for me. No 'in the rear with the gear.'"

He covered a few more paces, coming to the main hallway of O'Bannon, then turning with others into the reception area, near the foyer with the photos of the Medal of Honor winners.

"Well, look at your infantry monitor over there, Lee," said George. "That guy don't look like no hard charger to me!"

Lee Roy looked at the 0300 table, and it was as his friend had said. Most of the MOS monitor officers stood tall and straight. They were fit, and they beamed at the oncoming second lieutenants, with gazes suggesting heroism and courage. Frankly, thought Lee Roy, they looked like marine officers were supposed to look. All but the infantry monitor officer, who was short, fat, and apparently nervous. Lee Roy looked away. He didn't want it to be true. He looked back, and it was true. And he felt a burning shame.

Lee Roy didn't want anyone to see his flushed face, and he went to look at the other tables. He looked down at the pictures and the pamphlets, exchanged a few words with the model officers, and looked at their ribbons—the thin row of colors across the left breast, just above the campaign pocket of the uniform blouse. The ribbons told the stories of each man. They had all been there, Lee Roy could see. They all had campaign medals from Vietnam, the yellow Vietnam service ribbon that said they had been there, the green-and-white campaign ribbon that said they had stayed six months or more, the Combat Action Ribbon that said they had heard the sound of the guns, and the National Defense Service Medal that said that they had answered their country's call at a time when many young men in the United States had made their way to Canada or to Harvard Law School, or otherwise had evaded military service.

All these young marine officers had been there, thought Lee Roy, and he was awed.

The infantry table came up again; Lee Roy could not avoid it. He looked down at the infantry monitor, who had a strange, cherubic look about his ruddy face. Fat bulged over the white tunic collar of his dress-blue uniform. His eyes seemed apprehensive. He had two fingers of his right hand wedged inside the collar, and he was pulling it away from his neck.

An infantry captain, he wore the broad, silver "railroad tracks" across both shoulder epaulets.

"How do I look?" he asked Lee Roy. "Does my collar look okay?" The officer seemed anxious and insecure.

This was hard for Lee Roy. It wasn't right.

"Okay," said Lee Roy. "You look okay."

The infantry monitor seemed relieved. "Not too many guys are coming to my table," he said. "I wonder why?"

Then Lee Roy looked at his medals. The other monitors may have looked more brave and strong, but the infantry monitor had something they didn't have. He had two rows of campaign medals, like the others, and from a distance they looked the same. But above these the infantry captain had a small, single ribbon, sky-blue, with five white stars across it: the Medal of Honor. And then Lee Roy saw the deeper blue of a Purple Heart, with two stars. Three times this man had been wounded in combat against the enemies of the United States, and at least once he had all but given up his own life only to have it handed back to him, thought Lee Roy. The Medal of Honor was there on the chubby captain's chest.

Lee Roy looked toward the Medal of Honor wall where the pictures were. The portraits there didn't look like this guy in front of him. Lee Roy was trying to understand. Was this man a hero?

"Where did you get these?" asked Lee Roy, looking at the captain's medals.

"Vietnam," said the monitor. He said it quietly.

"What did you do?" asked Lee Roy awkwardly, wanting to point at the blue ribbon but knowing that would be wrong. "What did you do to get that one?" By Lee Roy's motioning with his head the captain understood what he meant.

The captain seemed uncomfortable again.

"You know," he said, looking about almost furtively, "the truth is, I don't have a good memory of a lot of it." He looked about again, as if he were ashamed—of the medal, or talking about it.

"That's not what I'm supposed to say here at The Basic School on MOS Day. But there it is." He turned away from Lee Roy and the other second lieutenants a bit, so that his ribbons were less visible to them. It was as if he didn't want the young lieutenants to see the blue one.

There were heroes pictured on the wall, and now here was a hero here in front of Lee Roy who was trying to understand it all.

He thought of the others who must have been with this captain that day that led to the blue medal. And Lee Roy saw briefly that some of those others must not have come back. Of course not. With a hero there must always be death, thought Lee Roy.

Death followed heroes like a shadow all through their lives. Lee Roy wondered about those others, but he could not know.

"Are you going into the infantry?" asked the captain. He had asked twice, and now Lee Roy heard him.

"Yes," said Lee Roy. "Yes." The captain had nothing to say to that, and Lee Roy moved on, to visit the supply officer.

Christmas Eve, 1967
Lubbock, Texas

Lee Roy Herron awoke early, before dawn. He lay still in his bed in the small Herron house in northeastern Lubbock. His eyes were open, and he stared up at the ceiling. Three small crosses, faintly luminescent, were fixed in a semicircle above him, plastic crosses glued to the ceiling. Danny had wanted the crosses there. She had given them to him at the end of their Thanksgiving holiday at LIFE Bible College. She had made a little joke about them, that Lee Roy should stick them on the ceiling above his bed and that they would be a blessing for him, whatever lay ahead in 1968, but that she was too short to make the blessing stick. That's what she had said. Lee Roy remembered her adding, "Only you can make the blessing stick, Lee Roy."

So Lee Roy had taken the crosses with him, back to The Basic School, and now he had brought them home to Lubbock. And here in the too-small room of his boyhood, Lee Roy had stood on the bed and stuck the crosses on the ceiling. Now he looked at them in the dark, and there was still a faint glow in them from light that had come to them the previous day.

Lee Roy listened for sounds in the house, or for the sound of wind outside, but all was quiet. He tried to feel it all—everything in this instant. He tried to grasp the moment and take it inside himself so he could hold it there forever, every detail: the white quilt askew across his boyhood bed, the quiet of the house before dawn, a feeling of peace. He held these things close so that he could take them with him where he was going.

There came a faint metallic sound, then the sound of the kitchen faucet and a cupboard door opening. Lorea was up, making coffee for the family on Christmas Eve morning as on every other morning. Slowly, quietly, Lee Roy sat up, got out of bed, and picked up his bathrobe from across the nearby chair. Quietly he opened the bedroom door and walked out to the kitchen.

"Hello, Ma," said Lee Roy, coming up behind her and placing his hands on her shoulders.

"Lee Roy!" she said, and she turned. "Here," she said, "have some coffee." She handed him a cup. "Sit in that chair." She pointed. "Your father and your sister aren't up yet, so we can talk here just like we used to do before you'd go to school."

Lee Roy sat. His mother had the gas stove on, and she was stirring batter, and it all went so smoothly, as effortlessly as the years had passed since he had sat in this very chair as a high school student, his mother laying bacon slices in the pan just as she had done then. But things were not the same, and would never be the same again. Time did that, thought Lee Roy. It took moments and passed over them, changed them, and made each one of them unique.

"I'm thinking of asking Danny to marry me," said Lee Roy. His mother continued with the mechanics of breakfast making, and now slid plates onto places at the table.

"What do you think of that?" asked Lee Roy.

"I pretty much figured that was coming," said Lorea. She was looking at him now. She had paused briefly, holding napkins in front of her.

"Yes," said Lee Roy. "But how do you know what's right? How do you know if it's the right thing to do?"

"You've always known what's right, Lee Roy," she said. She continued her smooth movements, now placing silverware, each utensil to its appointed place. "Sometimes I think you were born knowing what to do, Lee Roy," his mother said.

"I was thinking of asking her tonight," he continued. "At her house."

"This would be a fine night, under the Christmas Eve stars, to ask Danny to marry you," said Lorea.

And then Lee Roy's father; his sister, Jane; and her husband, Rhonald, were coming down the hallway, and the Herrons breakfasted together.

All year long West Texas sunsets are broad and red across the plains, and so it was this Christmas Eve when Lee Roy drove the family Fairlane the short distance to the Davis home. The radio played Christmas music: "Silent Night," "O, Come, All Ye Faithful," and "The Chipmunk Song," with Alvin, the troublemaking chipmunk, singing off key. Lee Roy was a jumble of thoughts and feelings, some of them at odds.

The Davis house was simple, neat, and white. Lee Roy parked in front, stepped out of the Fairlane, closed the door, and stood looking at the house for a time. There were colored Christmas lights strung across the eaves, and Lee Roy thought it the most beautiful sight of his life. He wondered if he should have worn his uniform. He had bought a navy blue sport coat in the exchange at Quantico, and was wearing it now with gray trousers, white shirt, and red tie. Lee Roy felt strange dressed this way.

"Are you coming in, Lee Roy?" asked Danny from the front door. She stood holding it open with one hand. Lee Roy looked up at her.

"Yes!" he said. "Sorry," he added quietly, so softly that Danny did not hear.

Inside, Danny's parents, Doc and Bennie, were beaming, happy to see Lee Roy. All their visitors meant a chance for them to learn something new, to make a new friend or renew friendships. Danny's father shook Lee Roy's hand and asked him about Quantico. Was it pretty tough there? Would Lee Roy be going to Vietnam? And wasn't it almost *over* over there—hadn't we about whipped the Vietcong?

Lee Roy stood smiling, saying nothing.

"Would you hush, Doc!" said Danny's mother. She took her husband by the hand and pulled him back.

"Lee Roy is not here to see us," she said. "Lee Roy is here to see Danny, and you and I are going to walk out now and visit the Jordans down the street like we told them we would."

Doc Davis smiled and nodded. He wore the denim overalls of a plains farmer, with a crisp white shirt and new black shoes. Lee Roy didn't think of it, but this was Doc dressed up—this was his Christmas outfit.

"Okay, Mother," said Doc. He had always called his wife that, it seemed. "I'll get your coat for you." And he lifted a red cloth coat from a row of wooden hooks in the hallway, handed it to Bennie, and they left.

Lee Roy and Danny stood there alone, facing each other. The top of Danny's head came only to Lee Roy's shoulders, but when she looked up at him and smiled she seemed just right to him.

"Shall we go into the living room?" asked Danny. She motioned. The living room was right there.

"Of course," said Lee Roy. He moved quickly, then realized that he should have let Danny go first, and it was awkward.

They sat down on a white couch, a distance apart. Lee Roy

looked about, and sat with his back straight and his hands on his knees.

"Would you like some tea?" asked Danny. Lee Roy did not know that she drank tea. At his house tea had been reserved for sick children, with brown sugar or honey added.

"Yes," said Lee Roy. "And could I have some brown sugar in it?" he said. He added, "I always take brown sugar in my tea."

"Of course," said Danny. She rose and went into the kitchen.

Lee Roy watched her move. Danny wore a Christmas sweater, red and green with a reindeer silhouette on the front. Her skirt was green, too, touching her knees, a bit longer than the fashion of 1967. She had a good figure, thought Lee Roy. If they got married, what would that mean, he wondered. He had never seen a naked woman except for two pictures that Charles Lance had shown him furtively while sitting in a high school assembly. What would it all mean?

Danny returned with the tea. Lee Roy sipped some, and looked at the Davis family's Christmas tree. It had small white lights, red glass balls, and green glass balls. Finally he turned to look at Danny.

She had short brown hair, clear brown eyes, and a pleasant smile, like Doc, her father. Danny's was a face, he thought, that he could wake up to for fifty years. She seemed sure of her faith, and sure of herself. And Lee Roy felt good when he was with her.

Danny and the Davis family seemed like steady beacons of light for the storms that Lee Roy knew lay ahead for him in 1968.

Lee Roy started to speak, not knowing what he would say. But Danny went first.

"The Lord has brought you here this Christmas Eve," she said. "I have given my life to the Lord, and he is showing me the way."

She sat forward on the white couch, with her knees slightly toward Lee Roy. Her look was eager and earnest, and her eyes met Lee Roy's without looking away.

"I put in for language school," said Lee Roy. "At Monterey." This wasn't exactly what he had meant to say, but there it was. "And I got it," he added. "I'm going to the language school that the army has. I finish The Basic School on January thirty-first, and I'll start the language school March second. It will last thirty-two weeks. I won't have to go over till after that."

"Where is it?" asked Danelle.

"Monterey is in California," said Lee Roy. "Up by San Francisco, I think."

"What does it mean, Lee Roy?" said Danny. She was eager. And she was relieved. A powerful wave of emotion moved through her.

"Does that mean you won't be—you won't be going over?" Danelle tried never to say "Vietnam." The closest she could bring herself was the phrase "over there."

"No," said Lee Roy. "Not for a year anyway. I won't be going for a year."

"That's so wonderful, Lee Roy," said Danelle. "That's so wonderful."

Danny put her hands on Lee Roy's knee. He wondered if he should kiss her, but he was afraid.

Suddenly Lee Roy felt ashamed, ashamed at what he had said, ashamed at what he had done. He had checked the box "Request Vietnamese Language School" on the MOS form, but he had never thought he would get it. It wasn't what he had always said he would do. He didn't know why he had done it. And now he was sitting here in the Davis house about to propose. This wasn't how it was supposed to be.

"Do you think," he began, and now he placed his hands on

top of Danny's, "Do you think it was . . . I mean, the others are going to Vietnam, and now I . . . Do you think I'm a—coward?" He almost couldn't say the word. Lee Roy's gaze turned down, away from Danny's eyes.

Now, for the first time ever, Danny slid herself close to Lee Roy, touching him, side to side, and she lay her head against him, and they both felt the warmth and goodness of this moment.

"How long does the language school last?" she asked, not remembering exactly what he'd said, her eyes closed now, her head still on Lee Roy's shoulder.

"Eight months," said Lee Roy.

"Oh, Lee Roy," said Danny. She snuggled even closer to him. And she took her arms from his knee and put them around his chest.

"The country needs you now, Lee Roy Herron, and I understand that." She spoke softly. "The Marine Corps needs you, and they will have you soon enough. I understand that."

Lee Roy looked at the Christmas tree with its white lights now grown soft and blurry from the tears that had come to his eyes.

"Maybe the Lord is giving us a year, Lee Roy. A year that wasn't ours, that we didn't deserve."

Lee Roy nodded.

"The Lord wants us to have this year, Lee Roy, and there's no point in our asking the why of it."

Lee Roy nodded again, but could not speak.

"The Lord has a purpose in this, Lee Roy," she said. "But we just cannot see it now."

After a time, Lee Roy spoke.

"Do you remember, Danny, we said that, when I came back, we might do something. You know. We might—" He couldn't finish it, couldn't get the words out.

"I remember," said Danny. "I remember what we said at Thanksgiving."

"Well," said Lee Roy, "I was thinking, since I'm going to language school for a year or so, and not Vietnam right away, I was thinking maybe—maybe we could be together for that year?"

"What are you saying, Lee Roy?" she asked.

"I mean, would you marry me?" he said. And he felt better. The words were out.

Danny's head turned just a bit, and her face right then might have shown many thoughts and feelings.

"Yes," she said simply, looking up at Lee Roy, looking into his eyes.

"We wouldn't be changing our plans that much," continued Lee Roy, now hurrying, as if to move quickly away from Danny's acceptance. "We wouldn't have children, like we said. And you're finished with college in May, and if anything happened, you could just say you had spent that time with me in Monterey." Danny placed her hands upon his knees again, and he was quiet.

"I said yes, Lee Roy. Yes."

"When?" asked Lee Roy.

"In May, just after I finish college," she said.

And then it was over. Neither of them knew what more to say.

Danny sat back, away from Lee Roy, so she could look up at him again.

"Call David Nelson," said Danny. "Tell him what we're going to do." Danny had a spiritual look on her face, the look she had when she spoke of LIFE College.

"I don't know," said Lee Roy. "He and Martie won't be at their apartment. I wouldn't know where they are."

"They'll be at her parents' house," said Danny. "I have the

number." She rose, hurried out of the room, and returned quickly with a piece of paper in her hand.

"See," said Danny. "And the telephone's right there, on the table." Indeed it was. The light-green plastic phone was one of Danny's parents' few concessions to modernity.

Lee Roy looked at Danny. Danny was so real, thought Lee Roy. So straight and clear and faithful.

"He wouldn't really—" Lee Roy took the paper but he did not look at it. "David Nelson is too—" And, not finding words to fit the moment, Lee Roy left it at that.

"You're inviting him to our wedding, aren't you?" continued Danny. Her eyes were open wide now, and her hands were clasped together, almost like she was praying. Lee Roy gave in.

"All right," said Lee Roy. "I'm calling him."

Lee Roy picked up the phone, dialed the number. He looked at Danny, who had sat back, more relaxed. "Direct dial," said Lee Roy. "Can you imagine?"

After a few seconds Lee Roy spoke into the phone.

"Is David Nelson there?" he asked. Danny was sitting by him, smiling. She was certain about all of this.

"Hello, David," said Lee Roy. There was some talking from the other side.

"I'm going—I mean I'm not going," said Lee Roy, and he was trying to find the right words. "I'm not going to Vietnam," he said. "I'm going to Language School."

Lee Roy listened for a moment.

"Vietnamese Language School, at Monterey," he said. "It's in California."

"Yes," said Lee Roy. "Right."

Danny wondered why Lee Roy was delaying mentioning the wedding.

Lee Roy Herron towers over his fiancée, Danelle Davis, soon after he proposed to her on Christmas Eve in 1967. Courtesy of the Herron family.

"There's something else," said Lee Roy. "No," he said. Then another no.

"David," said Lee Roy. "Danny and I are getting married." He seemed tense saying this.

"May fourth," said Lee Roy. "In Lubbock."

"I hope, we hope you can come, David," said Lee Roy. These words had come out the right way, thought Danny. This was important. "We both hope you can come, and Martie too," he said.

Lee Roy listened for a time. David was speaking.

"Are you sure?" asked Lee Roy. "It's only a five-hour drive." He listened again.

"All right," said Lee Roy. "I understand." After a time he hung up the phone.

"What's the matter?" asked Danny. "Isn't he coming?"

"He'll see," said Lee Roy. "Law school is really tough. He'll come if he can."

"Oh," said Danny.

"I think he was surprised to hear that we were getting married," said Lee Roy.

"Yes," said Danny.

"It wasn't what we had said last summer," said Lee Roy, and his words were soft, toned down, even.

"No," said Danny.

Lee Roy and Danny were married in the First Foursquare Church in Lubbock, just over four months later—and I wasn't there. The ceremony was small, I heard later. I had wanted to attend but I was facing a torts examination that weekend, a big exam for a first-year law student. I just couldn't go.

[8]
1968
The Will to Prepare

October 25

Southern Methodist University School of Law, Dallas, Texas

"Preparation," spoke Professor Abrams, as he strode first to the left and then to the right along his measured pathway at the front of the large lecture amphitheater in Florence Hall. "Preparation is the foundation of any successful legal action." He spoke scornfully, as if fully assuming that not one of the second-year law students in the tax-law class in front of him was prepared now, had ever contemplated preparation as a concept, or had any general intentions of preparation in the future. He looked to see if the students were listening. They were.

Professor Abrams was lecturing about tax law and municipal authorities. Boring.

"One of the few culturally syntonic statements that I have ever heard from one of your football heroes—" He paused, looked up again. The class dreaded his repetitive and disparaging remarks about football players, whom Professor Abrams used continuously as placeholder figures, like philosophers used Xanthippe, the much-maligned wife of Socrates.

"One of the few *reasonable* statements from one of your football heroes came from your counselor of the gridiron, Bear Bryant of Alabama." He continued to pace. As he accentuated the word "reasonable," some members of the class clenched their teeth.

"Now, said Counselor Bear is alleged to have stated to his football students that the will to win is common amongst football players, perhaps universal, but that the will to prepare"—and here he stopped, and turned directly toward the class—"the will to prepare is a rare thing."

Professor Abrams moved to the podium. The class was silent.

Clasping the edge of the podium with his small hands, he looked at the second-year law class spread across rows of wooden seats, the students wearing sandals, long hair, and colored beads. The bow-tie-wearing Professor Abrams did not approve. It was hard to tell the men from the women, he thought. Outside was the stately Georgian architecture of a great law school; inside was the rabble of the agora—and it was his task to make this rabble into attorneys.

"Mr. Nelson," he said in his baritone voice, not looking at me. "May I ask for your comments on Counselor Bear's argument?"

I stood up slowly from my third-row seat, and its varnished armrest creaked against aged hinges. I always wore a suit coat and tie, even though I only had two coats. I didn't want to be a member of the agora; it just seemed to turn Professor Abrams more adversarial.

In this case I was not prepared. I had been daydreaming, although I had heard the part about Bear Bryant. It had turned out that Martie's money from teaching was not enough to support us while I was in law school, and I had been thinking about that. I had also had trouble with my scholarship, which I had thought to be for all three years. In fact it was a performance-contingent scholarship, and I had lost it for my second year. This meant that Martie and I had had to borrow $1,400 for the second year, and this worried me. I needed some time after having been called on, and so I rose slowly.

"Strictly speaking," I began, standing straight now, facing my adversary at the podium, "the alleged statement of Mr. Bryant's is not an argument but a principle. There is no 'if this, then that' in the statement. No claim bearing upon facts, nor linking to facts in such a way that the logic of an argument could be assessed."

Professor Abrams did not take his eyes from me. He had been careless with words, and I had purchased some time, perhaps even discomfited him enough so that he would be off his own game, as it were, and would provide openings for me. And there was always the possibility he would turn to someone else.

"Let me refresh your memory, Mr. Nelson," he continued. I was relieved. He was going to restate the case facts that I had missed. I was saved. I felt the many eyes of the other students in the lecture hall.

"Let us recall," intoned Professor Abrams, "that for purposes of our discussion today, a wealthy and retired Dallas Cowboys football player has entered the real estate arena." Professor Abrams particularly loved the term "arena," which he used as a substitute for "venue" in tax law cases. Professor Abrams detested professional football players and considered them all wealthy, boorish, and predatory.

"And let us further assume that said football player has reaped large sums of money selling subprime mortgages to unwitting first-time homeowners throughout the State of Texas, while maintaining his home office in Plano, Texas, Collin County."

I closed my eyes partway, and far off I could see Staff Sergeant McNab in the squad bay of the PLC camp at Quantico. Whatever happened to me now and forever could never rival those days, and such a realization gave me comfort.

"And let us further assume that said Collin County, Texas, has recently enacted a municipal tax law, lawfully taxing any and all personal or business income which is derived from gainful activities which occur in that county." Professor Abrams stopped. He paused. He looked over the top of his glasses at me. I felt a surge of empathy for children in special education classes.

"I suppose I need not tell you, Mr. Nelson," continued Abrams, and he drew out the verb "tell" until it sounded like waves washing on a beach, "I need not tell you that there is now and increasingly will be a lot of *money* in Collin County, Texas"—dread overcame me here—"because the City of *Plano* is in said county"—and here I suddenly wondered who I was—"and where there is *money*"—and here there was a great pause—"there will be lawyers!" I thought Professor Abrams had sated his thespian urges, but he added: "Including yourself, Mr. Nelson. Including yourself." And it was temporarily over. The class was quiet. They could not yet see the road forward, could not see who would triumph, Professor Abrams or me.

I thought of the fat candidate whom Staff Sergeant McNab had intimidated that day in the corrugated-steel squad bay. I wondered where that candidate was, whether Staff Sergeant McNab had demolished his soul. In my mind, I could see the fat candidate now contentedly delivering mail or making change to customers at a dry-cleaning counter, and I thought how fortunate he would be, doing such jobs instead of standing here in front of Professor Abrams. These were dangerous thoughts when Professor Abrams had you cornered. I would have to recover. I forced my mind back to mortgages and football players. Luckily, I could count on at least one more Abrams soliloquy.

"But your client, the football player," continued Professor

Abrams in a tone of voice he had crafted over many years of lecturing on boring topics such as tax law, "your client has established a series of storefront satellite offices throughout the great state of Texas." Professor Abrams rarely just said "the State of Texas," and most of us believed that he had disdain for Texas, as we felt he had disdain for us. "And in these storefront offices he has positioned his employed representatives, mostly young women with blonde hair, blue eyes, and high school educations." Here Professor Abrams turned his head to the left; gender bias was frequently apparent in his speech and he had a vague feeling that this could cause him trouble one day. "And these said young women do rightfully accept the mortgage applications, and do dutifully collect the revenues from those applications each month." Here Professor Abrams paused and cast a malevolent eye upon the entire tax law class. "When the hardworking citizens who have signed these mortgages are *able* to make such payments," Professor Abrams added. He must be a Democrat, I thought.

He wasn't stopping. "At every collection said young women representatives forward said payments to the corporate office in Plano, but in said corporate office in Plano let us say that there is a whistleblower citizen—an honorable citizen such as yourself, Mr. Nelson." Professor Abrams paused, and even the backbenchers could feel the imputation that I might not be an honorable citizen, at least when things should come to tax law and its evasions. "An honorable citizen who reports to the municipal authorities of Collin County, Texas, that your football player client is evading and avoiding the payment of municipal income taxes rightfully due the said County Government." Here Professor Abrams stopped and looked down upon me squarely, like a preacher towering over a front-pew recalcitrant. I turned my head slightly, gazing at the exits. Time was up, I thought.

"Is the whistleblower correct, Mr. Nelson?"

"Intentionality," I said. I didn't know where that had come from, but immediately I felt saved. I thought of Lee Roy that moment, Lee Roy sitting in the fluorescent classrooms of the Department of Defense Language Institute in Monterey, and it made me feel better to think of him. I felt a bombastic surge of lawyerly triumph, and wondered briefly if I could have made it in the Yale Dramat.

"It depends upon the primary intention behind the establishment of the satellite offices of the real estate company," I said. "Whether that intention was to offshore the booking of mortgage revenues to other counties so as to avoid payment of Collin County municipal taxes, or whether that intention was to decentralize the company so as to enhance service and increase revenues."

There was silence in the amphitheater. Professor Abrams stood still. I had surprised myself. I thought of Lee Roy again, and I sensed that while what I was facing was a game, what Lee Roy was facing was real. I felt ashamed that I had even been riled about it.

Professor Abrams paused behind the lectern, his mouth opened just so, and a glint of a few small white teeth appeared. This was a good sign. Staff Sergeant McNab had been worse, I thought. But then there was a doubt. What about Vietnam? What about Lee Roy? It was all confusing.

"Are you then a Cartesian?" asked Professor Abrams. There was a brief snicker in the class, from high up, in the safety of the back rows. Then there was laughter. Professor Abrams opened his mouth wider, and the gold of one incisor showed through. It would be all right, I thought. It would be all right now. It was a Friday, this was the last class of the day, and Professor Abrams had shown the gold tooth: very favorable. But I laid more on— served some more pork, as we said in those days.

"In the end," I continued, riding a flow of laughter from the back benches, "all law rests upon the subjective will of the people, expressed in the opinions of courts and legislatures." I did frighten myself there. That had been a bit much. The class laughed again. Professor Abrams closed his eyes and shook his head. "Class dismissed for the weekend!" he said. And there was a great rumbling of books and creaking of armrests and shuffling feet.

I put my books and notes in my briefcase, an old one I had gotten in Lubbock, while the other students filed out into the hall, past the oil portraits of prominent SMU alumni on the wall. Sometimes on Friday afternoons I wanted the hall to clear out some before I walked out there. But when I walked out that day, some students were still there, talking in small groups, a buzzing of voices, weekend relief in everyone's manner.

Joyce was standing across from the lecture hall door. It wasn't obvious that she was waiting for me, but I think she was. Joyce was from Houston, married, an older law student, not right out of college like the rest of us. I wasn't sure what she had done in those years after college, or how many years there had been. Joyce was not really attractive to me, though she was interesting. And she liked me. That was it, really. She liked me.

She came up to me that Friday after class, I remember. Long blond hair, tight sweater, jewelry dangling, a little overweight. That was Joyce, I thought. Her skirt had a crinkled, chiffon texture to it. And it was short, very short. I tried not to look at it, as I recall. Don't go there, I thought. I tried to look at her eyes.

"I thought you were great in there today, Mr. Nelson," said Joyce.

What it was about Joyce, looking back on it, was that she could see something in me. She had an unconditional positive regard for me, as if she saw something in me that she wished was in her husband, or something like that. At least that's what I thought at the time. I wondered about her husband sometimes; she never mentioned him. I knew Joyce was married, and it made me uncomfortable when she came up close to me.

"Oh, Joyce," I said. "I don't think so, Joyce." I always swung around, and sometimes away, when Joyce came close. I must have appeared clumsy to her. It was time to go home anyway. My Ford Falcon was waiting for me in the parking lot. I thought of the Falcon sometimes like it was a person or a pet. I felt I should go to it, but Joyce was there.

"How do you know so much about the law?" Joyce asked. There was a faint but clear feeling of sunshine and flowers about her. I was never sure if that was Joyce's perfume or if that was her. She held her books in front of her so there was a boundary between us. I thought of Lee Roy and how nothing that was happening to me was of any consequence compared with what he was doing.

"I wouldn't have known what to say if Professor Abrams had called on me. I just wouldn't have known," she said.

"Oh, Joyce," I said.

"Hey, gyrene!" came a sudden, mocking duet of discordant voices from a wooden bench across the hall. ("Gyrene," a term—like "jarhead"used by marines—was generally derogative when used by civilians.) I turned away from Joyce. Across from us sat Mike and Pat, law students who came from somewhere in East Texas, perhaps near Tyler. Someplace where everybody might be retarded or have neurosyphilis, I thought then. But I smiled.

To me, Mike and Pat—I never did know their last names—were not really law students. They didn't look like law students, didn't act like law students, and could only have become such through some structural lacuna in the algorithms that had been used by the Admissions Committee of the SMU School of Law, thereby wreaking untold and successive waves of mischief against the good order of the legal world into the distant future. Mike and Pat had long, dirty hair. They were slobs, I thought. I smiled.

"Did you hear the one about the guy who wanted to avoid the draft?" said one of them, speaking as if to an audience in the hallway.

"No!" said the other. "Do tell me how, because that's what I would like to do-o-o."

"Well," said the first, and now he had a small audience, some members of the class who dressed and acted similarly. To me they looked like a faded painting of the twelve disciples I had once seen on a wall in a church basement, but without the disciples' dignity.

"Well, this guy decided to join the Marine Corps, so when the draft board met they said, 'We can't get 'im—he's in the marines!'"

"Like David Nelson, ya mean?" asked the other, fingering a bronze peace sign that hung around his neck on a leather cord, flapping against the words "Peace Now" across the front of a cut-off sweatshirt. I thought briefly of Lee Roy, wearing a Marine Corps uniform in California, and I worried about the welfare of America.

"Just like David Nelson!" said the other, and then he laughed like a hyena: "Ha-hee, ha-hee, ha-hee!"

I smiled at them. They turned away. It was time to go.

"Pay no attention to them," Joyce said. She stood still. She always waited for me to leave first.

"I'll see you next week," I said, and I turned to go.

"Goodbye, David," she said.

• • •

The drive between Irving, where Martie and I lived, and the SMU School of Law in Dallas was twenty miles each way, and I drove it daily. These were the days of low gasoline prices, but it was still a stretch on our budget.

I was fond of my light-blue 1960 Falcon. It had an inline, six-cylinder engine and a three-speed stick shift on the steering column. The stick had so much slack in it that it was hard to know what gear you had found until the Falcon moved, bucked, or gave some other clue. It didn't have an air conditioner, and the heater didn't work well, but the car always started, and I don't recall ever missing a day of law school.

We didn't do much during those years, Martie and I. Sometimes I look back on it, and I can't recall details. There was a long stretch of days and months—years—filled with commuting, studying, eating simple dinners with Martie from TV trays, and shopping and cleaning on weekends. In its way, at times, law school seemed like the Hill Trail. It was something you just had to do or you couldn't come out the other end.

Martie's parents visited us sometimes, and they would take us out to dinner at the restaurant of our choice, a special treat for us. One time, I remember, we had all gone out to dinner at a seafood restaurant in the center of Irving. Afterward we walked along the sidewalk, window-shopping, and Martie saw a yellow leather purse in the window, and she liked it. Martie's father took me aside and offered to give me the money to buy it for her, but I refused.

I don't know why I did that. Martie wasn't getting much during those years. I just didn't have much to give her. And then, when I had the chance to buy her the yellow purse, I didn't do it. Afterward I had regrets.

These thoughts and others were heavy in my mind that Friday

as I drove home to Irving. Usually I felt a general uplift on a Friday afternoon, a feeling that one more week of law school was behind me, a feeling that there was progress, but not today. The yellow purse was in my mind. I felt I could see it looking back at me from the store window, mocking me, accusing me of penury and of being a failure as a husband. I felt I had made a mistake about that purse.

I was actually considering quitting law school that day. As the Falcon rumbled home, I felt like I just couldn't do it anymore. There was just too much law school and not enough of anything else.

I was unaware of time passing until I felt the Falcon slow down, and I realized I was in the parking lot of the apartment building where Martie and I lived. I sat behind the wheel for a time, I remember. It was hard to open the door and to get out. Earlier I had decided to become an accountant—I had majored in accounting at Texas Tech, and there were jobs in that field. Of course, there was the problem of the Marine Corps. I had taken the commission at graduation, and there would be a three-year obligation to them. But they needed accountants, I told myself. At least I would be paid, and we would have a house to live in on base.

I got out of the Falcon, walked with my briefcase to the glass front door of the apartment building, and inserted my key. The steps to the second floor, where we lived, were open, without balustrades behind them, and I could see second-floor apartment doors. Martie was there, I knew she would be there. She always was there to open the door for me. Before I could reach for my key in my pocket, the door opened to our apartment. Martie stood in the doorway, smiling at me, without a word.

I had a routine when I arrived home. I carried my briefcase

into the bedroom, and I changed my clothes. I hung my suit coat, shirt, and trousers in the closet, and I put on jeans, a T-shirt, and old tennis shoes. The apartment had just the one bedroom, and a sitting room, a small dining room table, and a kitchen separated by a half wall.

But this Friday I didn't go into the bedroom. I just sat down immediately on the couch we had. And Martie sat down next to me.

"What is it?" she asked.

"Martie," I said, but I did not look at her.

"Yes," she said.

"Martie," I said again. "I don't think I can make it."

I hadn't meant to put it so straightforwardly.

"We just can't make it, not for another year and a half. I just didn't make enough money in the warehouse last summer. We fall behind, more each month. We had to borrow fourteen hundred dollars for my tuition this year. It's my fault." I was getting more intense about it. I couldn't help it. I hadn't spoken about it for days, though I'd been thinking about it, and now that I had started it all came out.

"It's my fault because I lost the scholarship. I didn't know." Now I was turning to her.

"I didn't know the scholarship was dependent on a three-point average. I just didn't know." I turned away again, but I knew I wasn't done. Martie said nothing, but she did put her hand on my arm, I remember. She put her hand on my arm.

"The worst thing," I was forcing myself to finish, to get it all out. "The worst thing—is the yellow purse." Now I put my hands on her hands, and looked straight and clear into her eyes. "I was wrong about that, Martie! That was terribly wrong! I should have gotten that for you! I just didn't—we just didn't have anything."

I was not looking at her now. I remember looking at the carpet and seeing the browns and yellows in the weaving threads, and thinking that even the carpet was crap, artificial, hopeless.

"I can't work anymore and still do law school, Martie." All my protests at our existence were coming out.

"I tried that, Martie. I tried that. I just can't work in the warehouse and do the law school both." I was getting to the end. I tried to think of anything else I could complain about. I thought of Mike and Pat. I thought about Joyce. Of them I said nothing.

I tried to cry, looking down at the carpet, but I couldn't make tears come. Then I felt worse for trying.

Martie said nothing for a time. She had let her right hand come to rest along the top of my left leg.

"I feel that way sometimes, too, David," she said. "I feel that way, too." I could tell she meant it, even though I had not been aware of this before.

"The students aren't easy at Bowie Junior High, David," she said. "Sometimes I think they would just as soon burn the school down as go to it," she said. (Later, when I was at The Basic School, we heard that students *had* burned down Bowie Junior High School.)

"I try to teach them Texas history, and do you know, David, many of them don't care—they really don't care about it, whether they know anything about Texas history or not." Martie paused. I looked at her, and her eyes were very intense, widened and bright.

"At first, I thought they didn't have ability. I thought that must be it. They're incapable, and they weren't fed well when they were little, and maybe they just don't have the ability. That's what I told myself." I started to listen more carefully—to understand what Martie was telling me.

"Later, after a time, I came to realize that that wasn't it, David." Her hands tensed, and she drew them back from me and clasped them in her lap.

"I came to realize that they didn't care whether they knew Texas history, or math, or English literature, or anything. They really didn't care."

Now tears came to Martie's eyes, and her voice cracked some, and I put my hand on her shoulder.

"Do you know what that's like for a teacher, David?" Martie wasn't complaining. She was just telling.

"Some days," she continued, "I get to the fourth period, after lunch, and I don't think I can do it. I don't think I can finish the fifth and sixth periods.

"Some days I don't think I can go on," she said.

I was listening to her. I realized that I had not understood this. I had not taken enough care to understand Martie's feelings, I was realizing.

"That happened yesterday, David," she said. Her voice was even and steady. "I put my head down on my desk before fourth period, because I thought the students wouldn't be in the room yet, wouldn't see me." I looked up at her now. I was seeing things new about Martie.

"But one of the students did see me." She was looking straight into my eyes, and she placed her hands back against mine. "It was one of the boys, David. One of the boys who I thought cared nothing about the class or about me." I waited. "Maybe the worst one of the boys I have. He disrupts the class. He fights with other children. I dislike him. And then I thought, 'Oh, no!' Now he has seen me like this. It will make things all the worse!"

I hadn't considered this, how it must be for Martie at that junior high school.

"But I was wrong, David. I was wrong about him." Her visage was brightening. I didn't understand.

"He came up to me, and I was ashamed in front of him. He didn't come too close to me, but he stood near the desk, nearer the teacher's desk than he ever was before, and he asked me if I was okay."

Martie was crying now. The tears were coming, and I had not seen them since we had moved to Irving.

"The boy said he would teach my fourth-period class, David. An eighth grader, who refuses to take the tests in Texas history, who comes late to class, who gets sent to detention regularly. He said he would teach the class."

Martie did not wipe her tears. She let them come, and they streamed down her cheeks. I reached over and I touched one.

"And I let him teach the class, David. I watched from the back of the room, and he stood up in front, and he called on the children to talk about the Alamo, just like me, and the other children went right along with it." The tears were still coming, some. I could not think of anything to say, even though I had the idea from Professor Abrams that lawyers were always supposed to have something to say.

Martie was quieter now. She was working in her own mind to understand what had happened.

"What I realized then was—" She cried more, and she paused.

"What I realized then was that I don't understand things. Not my students. Not things in themselves. Not whether what we're doing now is right or important." Tears were streaming down her cheeks again. "And you don't either, David. What's going on with us, and what's going on out there in this crazy world," and she swept her hand toward the window across from us, against the chaos and violence of 1968. "We just have to go on, and follow the road as it comes to us."

Martie Nelson helps an unidentified marine lieutenant colonel pin on David Nelson's first lieutenant silver bars in a brief ceremony at the Naval Air Station, Grand Prairie, Texas, in September 1968. Official U.S. Marine Corps photo.

Martie seemed to feel better after saying these things.

"My student," she said. "I thought he didn't care about history or class or me or anything. But he did, David. He cares about everything," she said.

I looked away. I looked out our sitting room window. I couldn't understand it all.

"Do you think an eighth-grade delinquent boy can be a hero?" Martie asked. "I never thought so," she said, "but yesterday I thought so.

"So, you see," said Martie, "it doesn't really matter about the yellow purse. The yellow purse is not what counts."

Fall was coming, and outside we could see its orange colors in the late-day sunlight.

"Someday," Martie said, "someday, I'll have a lot of purses. But if I have no more days like yesterday, I'll be the worse for it."

We sat there for a time. It was better now, and I felt again like I could do law school. If my wife could teach junior high, and if a delinquent boy could teach a history class, I could do law school.

Martie felt better, too, I could tell.

"If you want to get a few extra dollars, David, why don't you go in with those two other law students who do roofs? You could help them on weekends, when there is time. And if you feel too stressed, you don't have to do it."

I liked that idea. I placed my arm around Martie's shoulders and drew her closer to me. Looking back on those years now, I wish that I had done that more. She laid her head against my arm.

October 25, 1968

Department of Defense Language Institute,
Monterey, California

Fifteen hundred miles to the northwest, on the eastern edge of the Monterey peninsula, close by the beaches of Carmel, Lee Roy Herron sat in a red plastic chair under fluorescent lights in a classroom of the U.S. Department of Defense Language Institute.

The room was too large, too bright, and too plastic for its assigned purpose, the conduct of small-group tutorials in the languages of the enemies of the United States. There were echoes in the room, the walls were thin plasterboard, and black-and-white photos of old military officers were hanging crooked on the walls.

The institute had been designed and built in the Presidio compound along with many other facilities like it during World War II. Generations of young officers had occupied its rooms, as had certain senior enlisted men, too many to be remembered, all transient, spending a few weeks or a few months until their orders had come to ship out. The Pacific lay waiting outside the boundary wire of the compound, and the young men could see it as they walked between the buildings.

Lee Roy sat in the front row. He sat in the same seat each day, a little off center, in front of a plywood lectern. Outside, through the windows, Lee Roy could see the sunshine, and other steel buildings like the one in which they sat. In front of him Mr. Bai stood and spoke in Vietnamese.

There were perhaps twenty young company-grade officers in the room. Most were army. Two or three wore the winter service tunics of the Marine Corps. On Lee Roy's tunic he wore the red-and-yellow National Defense Service Ribbon and, under it, the squared-off silver badges of those who had qualified as marksmen on the rifle and pistol ranges.

That bothered Lee Roy, the marksman shooting badges. It was never stated clearly at The Basic School, but everyone understood that infantry officers were expected to have expert shooting badges or, at worst, the intermediate sharpshooter badges. These things were more than symbolic in 1968. Soon most of those infantry lieutenants would be firing those rifles and .45 pistols at other human beings in Asia, and there was a big difference between hitting a target and just missing. Lee Roy blamed his low-but-passing grade on his glasses.

The instructor, Mr. Bai, was short and deferential, with a melodic tenor voice. Lee Roy was not sure about the many syllables of his full name. When Mr. Bai ate in the officers' club lunchroom, he always ate hurriedly, as if afraid he would be interrupted. Perhaps as a result of eating too many meals this way, he had become fat. Sometimes the students called him Mr. Phu Bai, after the big marine combat base in Quang Tri, and during breaks in the hallway they mocked his ways as students have always done when forced to sit in classrooms too long. Laughing at Mr. Bai reassured them somehow, because he was the first Vietnamese person they had met, and they had made the mistake of stereotyping. How hard could a war be against small people

Lee Roy Herron proudly wears his dress greens just after completing The Basic School for marine officers in early 1968. Courtesy of the Herron family.

with melodic voices who ate their lunches too fast? Unspoken was the certainty that there were Vietnamese across the sea who were not like Mr. Bai, and who were waiting for them. But no one ever said this.

The students read aloud with Mr. Bai. "Qui duc Lac," he intoned, then "Que duc Tho," then "Qua duc—" Whatever, thought Lee Roy to himself. He looked about the room. All the young men wore the winter service uniforms of the army or Marine Corps. All had combat arms ratings. After seven months in the school, not one of them could really speak, read, or write the Vietnamese language, nor did any of them much care. And it really won't matter, thought Lee Roy. Where we are going, it won't matter.

Lee Roy looked out the window again, toward the patches of the blue Pacific that he could just glimpse. He treasured these brief views of Monterey Bay. They were beautiful to him. He wanted to remember the bay's azure shade. Sometimes Lee Roy made a point of taking the measure of every moment during inconsequential times in the classroom, and to grasp and hold onto them, take them prisoner. He had come to realize that when he did this it was because there was fear behind it, fear of the passing time, and fear of what would soon be coming. Lee Roy did not like fear, and so he looked back to Mr. Bai and threw himself into the world of "duc" and "tho." He was a marine officer now, he told himself, and he had to jam every piece of knowledge into his brain, in case it should be needed.

And then the class session was over, the day was over, and another week was done. They would all have two days off. They would be like normal men for a few weeks more, with five-day workweeks, clean clothes, and weekends and evenings with wives and girlfriends. These were precious times to all of them, married and unmarried, officer and enlisted man.

There were five weeks to go for them in the language school. Lee Roy started to count the weekends left, and then he stopped.

The officer of the day entered the classroom. The young men all stood at attention beside their plastic chairs.

"Be seated; orders are in," said Captain LaFrance.

The young officers were rapt in their respect for Captain LaFrance, who stood in front of them, fit and tall, in the khaki working uniform of the army: short sleeves, lightweight trousers, silver belt buckle, the shirt taut across the muscles of his chest. Colored ribbons in three rows across his left breast pocket told the young officers that he had been in four campaigns in Vietnam. There was a unit commendation medal, the Bronze Star,

the Silver Star, and—at the top, in the center of the third row—
the midnight darkness of the Purple Heart. Captain LaFrance had
been there, been in numerous battles, received high medals for
valor, and returned alive. The officers in the Vietnamese language
program looked at him, and they knew that soon they would be
where he had been.

"When I call your name, come up and get your orders. Endorse
the originals where the stamp is, and leave those with me. I will
see that your final checks are cut from these, before you go on
terminal leave. The copies you should keep in your permanent
files."

"Terminal leave." It was just the way the army talked, thought
Lee Roy.

Captain LaFrance always spoke in a calm, measured voice, as
if nothing could ever upset him after what he had been through,
yet his tone suggested power, even lurking violence. He called
officers' names, and one by one each man walked to the front in
silence, signed his orders, and kept a copy. No one spoke, except
the recurring short command of the captain: "Sign here." The
others were quiet because they knew what their orders would
say. It was 1968, and the great North Vietnamese offensives that
had begun with Tet were continuing to roll through Quang Tri
and Quang Nam provinces.

Lee Roy looked at his orders. Through the dense, crafted word
rituals of the military, he knew where to look for what it really
meant, in the first paragraph, where he saw the words, "You are
hereby assigned to report to 'CG 3d Mar Div III MAF WestPac.'"
Lee Roy signed the originals of the orders, Captain LaFrance collected them, and Lee Roy walked back toward his seat. At his
chair, when he thought others might not notice, Lee Roy looked
down again at the first paragraph of the orders. The 3rd Marine

Division. He was going to I Corps. The 9th Marines, the 3rd Marines, the 4th: these were the regiments that were on the DMZ.

Lee Roy picked up his Vietnamese language book and some papers from his chair. He walked to the doorway, took his folded garrison cover from a hook on the wall, and looked at it, holding the soft wool hat in his hand for a moment. The black globe and anchor were there, on the right side of the cover, and the silver first lieutenant's bar on the left. He placed it on his head, snug and sharp, and he glanced at himself in the glass of the door. For a moment he thought he saw the face of Lieutenant Hawkins, the posthumous Medal of Honor winner at Tarawa in 1943, with scars across his face from a burn in his youth.

Lee Roy turned his head, opened the door, and walked out toward the sun that was low in the western sky. As he walked across the parade grounds of the school toward the transient officers' quarters, two enlisted men passed him, and Lee Roy saluted them smartly. He liked that, the sharpness of the salutes and the rituals of respect, the "good morning, sir," and the "good afternoon, sir." Things were in order here. Things made sense. Outside, the world and the nation were in turmoil, thought Lee Roy. But here, where they were together with the uniforms and the rituals, things were in order. Danny would be waiting for him across the Presidio, and Lee Roy walked toward her with the WestPac orders in his hand.

The transient officers' quarters (TOQ) at the Defense Language Institute looked the same as all the other buildings. There were three of them: steel walls against sparse grass, pale yellow paint, and windows that could be opened from the inside or the outside. The Defense Department had built them quickly as World War II ended, and they had left it to future generations to make each building unique. Later the interiors of the three buildings had been remodeled, divided into rows of small apartments, each the same, each with one small bathroom, one bedroom with a closet, and a kitchen that was little more than an annex to a sitting room. All looked the same, more or less, to someone walking by outside, or to a visitor. Lee Roy stopped in front of the short walkway to Number 43C. This one was special. In this apartment, he and Danny had had seven months together; Lee Roy walked over to language school in the morning and back to their apartment at the end of the day. Danny and Lee Roy had pretended that it was forever.

Lee Roy pulled open the screen door, then the glass-paneled wooden door to 43C. Danny was sitting on the sofa that stretched along the window, which looked out onto Monterey Bay. She was always there when Lee Roy came home. Sometimes she would be reading the Bible, sometimes other books. Lee Roy liked it that she was always there.

Danny looked up at Lee Roy. She could tell by the way he stood, and the papers in his hand. "The orders came, didn't they, Lee Roy?" she asked.

Lee Roy did not speak, but he moved his left hand partly upward, the hand that held the folded pages.

"Well, why don't you change your clothes," she said. "Just because some pieces of paper have come, I don't see why we should let it change anything here."

Lee Roy nodded.

"Go ahead now, Lee Roy," said Danny. "No," she said. "I don't need to see them." And Lee Roy turned and moved into the bedroom, where the green of the peninsula mountains was visible through the window.

"I saw Andy Vaart at the break today," Lee Roy called back. "He wants to know if we want to go with him and his girlfriend to a seafood restaurant in town, to have dinner. You know, Friday night and all."

"No," said Danny. "Why don't we just stay in tonight?" She held a Bible in her hand. "We can take a walk after dinner, down by the gate where we can see the bay, and we can look out at the water."

"Okay," said Lee Roy, changing into a sport shirt and slacks. Even his leisure clothes, he thought, were the colors of the Marine Corps summer uniforms.

He could see east from the bedroom, across rows of corrugated-steel buildings, past the gate and the concertina wire along the top of the boundary fence to the blue of the bay, and Lee Roy felt the wire dividing two worlds. That's just how it was, he thought. There was an inside and an outside, and there would be no way to go back across that line. No way for him and Danny to get out of it now, to flee into the mountains and hide in a cabin forever. No. The only way to cross that line now was straight ahead, out through the transport planes at Travis Air Force Base, and through whatever waited for him in Southeast Asia. That was the only way to cross the line between where he and Danny were and the blue bay beyond the wire.

Lee Roy hung his uniform carefully on hangers, lining the creases of the trousers just so. In the other room, Danny had gone from sitting on the couch to kneeling beside it. She was not looking at him as he emerged from the bedroom, but out through the window and across the hillsides to the bay. And in front of her on the couch was her Bible. Lee Roy knelt next to her. He placed his hands together, but he did not bow his head. Both of them looked out across the wire.

"I didn't have to go, you know," said Lee Roy, still looking out the window, kneeling next to Danny. "With my grades in language school I could have gone to Washington. I could have been a translator." He was thinking. He was remembering, trying to understand it all.

"I don't know why I did that," he said.

"You had to go, Lee Roy," said Danny. She had her eyes closed, her hands clasped tightly. "You had to go, Lee Roy," she said again, and they both knew that somehow that was true.

"God is calling to us now, Lee Roy," she said. "It is his will which will be done in what lies ahead," she said, Lee Roy close to her. She was not exactly praying, but it was something like that.

"We must not be afraid," Danny said. Lee Roy nodded. "He will not ask of us anything that we do not have to give," she said. Lee Roy nodded again. They knelt side by side, and they looked out across the bay to the mountains in the distance.

Lee Roy Herron (right) receives a trophy for high grades at the Department of Defense Language Institute, Monterey, California, October 1968 (names of other two men unknown). Courtesy of the Herron family.

[9]
December 1968
Goodbye, Farewell

I felt bad about missing Lee Roy and Danny's wedding, but Martie and I had no money, and I had to study for and take the torts examination. I was concerned because I had flunked the first-semester torts exam.

I had always believed that things like missing Lee Roy and Danny's wedding could be made up, fixed. That's what I told myself as Christmas approached in 1968. My experience has been that Christmas can be a time to bring things together, package them up, and I had a feeling that maybe Lee Roy and I would get together one more time before he went overseas. Maybe we would even sit by the playa lake like when we were boys, and talk things over, even come to some mutual understanding. I didn't see why everything had to change. I didn't realize then that things do change, and they pass away from you, and you cannot get them back.

The first problem with this idea about a Christmas get-together was that I was just too busy to go home to Lubbock. My final examinations went right up to December 23, and I felt it was so important that I do well on them, so I might get my scholarship back, that I worked all the time at getting ready for them. I also needed every additional hour I could squeeze out of my schedule for my roofing job with my two law school friends, because Martie and I needed every dollar I could make. This was the midpoint in my law school curriculum, and we were $1,700 in debt. I talked with Martie about it some, although she didn't seem that worried.

Then, coming up to the examinations, I got sick, and it was bad. Everything ached. I had fevers. Life became a blur of property law and tax law and night sweats; the misery became almost unendurable. I heard later that this illness was called the Hong Kong flu, and all I could think was that there wasn't much of anything that came from Asia that I liked.

I didn't have time to think of Lee Roy. I couldn't call him, because of the long distance charges. And I told myself that I didn't know where he was anyway. I had heard that he had shipped over before Christmas. Everything was just too much for me as 1968 came to an end.

Martie said that we had to go to her family's house for Christmas, the Lowry home in Temple. But she then said that if I was just working the way I was, she might as well go there on her own, and two days before Christmas she did. I stayed in Irving to finish my law school tests, and then I just lay in bed in our apartment, alone and exhausted. I know now that Martie and I were about at our limits that year. We had nothing left to give, financially or otherwise, sometimes even to each other. I was sure that Lee Roy would understand when finally we would sit by the playa lake again and look back on it all.

I felt a little better on Christmas Day, so I got out of bed, got the Falcon going, and drove to the Lowry home in Temple, one of those southwestern towns that grew up alongside the railroad. Its people serviced trains and sold food and drinks to the passengers; later there were hotels and stores, and then a great medical clinic grew, the Scott and White clinic, which is still there.

Martie's parents—Martie G. and Ruby Lowry—always cooked a big Christmas lunch and had gifts under the tree, and Martie's widowed aunt, LaVerne Carlile, came. They had a present for me, and I ate lunch, but somehow I wasn't happy. Things were not right in the world as 1968 ended. Bad things were coming, I just had a feeling about it. If you're a lawyer and an accountant, what are you supposed to do with feelings like that?

December 19, 1968
Lubbock, Texas

"Whoooo-eeee!" shouted Lorea Herron as the MGB convertible careened around the corner of the perimeter road in Lubbock and onto Slide Road. "You got this thing up on two wheels!" She screamed above the rattling four-cylinder English engine and the wind.

"No way, Mother!" shouted Lee Roy, turning the wheel and smiling broadly.

At Nineteenth Street he accelerated, weaving in and out of the two southbound lanes, and Lorea closed her eyes and let herself go—into the sun, the wind, the rattling of the engine—until she felt that she was disappearing. The MG roared and bucked at every intersection, and then they were below Sixty-eighth Street, where Lubbock ended at that time and where cotton fields took over the landscape and stretched forever to the horizons south and west.

"Stop there, Lee Roy!" screamed Lorea as they neared a broad, open space stretching to the west from Slide. Perhaps construction vehicles had made this space or perhaps cotton farmers. It didn't matter. They stopped, the car facing west, and Lee Roy turned off the engine. The young man and his mother were alone there, under the sunshine, looking out across the entire Southwest, it seemed.

"This car is so great, Lee Roy!" said Lorea, still shouting through the wind. She looked around at the car. It was cloud-blue on the outside, with a soft beige interior, and hammered-chrome face-plates across the dashboard. Lee Roy was looking at his mother and smiling broadly.

"Do you think it's over the top?" he asked. "The car, I mean." The smile lines disappeared and he looked concerned. "I didn't really need it. A sports car, and all. I never saw you and Dad waste money on something like this."

Lorea felt many things. She remembered how this boy had sometimes felt self-conscious at Christmas if he had gotten a gift that he especially liked. She remembered how he had once given his jacket to a poor boy at recess in the elementary school, because he had felt bad that that boy did not have one. She remembered many similar things.

"No, Lee Roy," she said. "You needed this car, and Danny will need it in California to wrap everything up out there."

The great sorting of time and chance was close upon them now, and Lorea wanted to see Lee Roy smile again.

"Do you remember, Lee Roy, the time you got the steak knife out of the drawer when your father and I were in the yard, and you were real little, and you went around to all the windows cutting the pull strings with the knife, to show that you knew what a knife was for?"

They both laughed, and Lorea saw her son smile, and she placed that smile carefully in her memory. But the smile faded as Lee Roy thought of his tearful goodbyes with Danny in California a few days before. She had chosen to stay in Monterey to take care of moving and other matters before returning to Lubbock.

Lee Roy and his mother sat there for a time, looking out across the cotton fields. "Good luck where you're going over there, Lee

Roy," said his mother. She gazed far across the western plains and spoke softly, not her usual voice.

"Thanks," said Lee Roy.

"I'm not going to say goodbye at the airport tomorrow, Lee Roy," she said, now in her normal voice, the voice of a Texas mother speaking to her young son, and teaching him what's right and true.

"No," she said. "I'm saying goodbye here in the MGB, where it's sunny and pleasant and we can see the whole state of Texas. Then I'm not going to speak of it again."

"Yes, Mother," said Lee Roy.

"Jane will stop by this afternoon to say goodbye," said Lorea. "She's pregnant, now, and she's a little weepy sometimes," she said.

"Fine," said Lee Roy.

"Tomorrow at the airport we're going to pretend we're just driving you down for a little trip, like we have done before. Just taking you to the airport. Nothing special or unusual about it."

"Yes," said Lee Roy.

"And there's not going to be any crying, or any of that nonsense tomorrow," Lorea said. "I'm just going to walk in with you, help you check your suitcase, and then I'll give you a hug, and say, 'Let us know when you're coming home again. We'll be here to meet you.'"

Lee Roy said nothing to this.

"That's how it's going to be tomorrow," said Lorea.

There were some little dust devils in the distance, waltzing and pirouetting their way across the vast cotton fields, small versions of their larger tornado cousins.

"There's something else I want to tell you, Lee Roy," said Lorea after a time. "It's about your father."

Lee Roy looked straight ahead.

"He probably won't be coming to the airport tomorrow, Lee Roy," she said. "He'll say it's because he's got to work at the station."

Some moments passed.

"And I know that from time to time he's been hard on you, Lee Roy," said his mother.

"But he's not coming to the airport tomorrow because he loves you so much. He loves you too much. He couldn't say it to you, but I'm saying it."

Tears came out now and rolled down Lorea's cheeks. Lee Roy, too, felt his vision glisten, and he could not see the sky. He took his glasses off and rubbed them against his shirt, as if the glasses were the problem.

"That's why your father won't be coming to the airport tomorrow, Lee Roy. I wanted to make sure you knew," said Lorea. And it was over.

Lee Roy started up the engine of the new sports car, and they headed back north on Slide Road, going home, now much more slowly.

The next day, December 20, came windy and cold, with low clouds moving south across the land, and dust in the air. Lee Roy had been up early, packing his suitcase, the gray-green plastic, folding valise that Marine Corps officers were issued in those years. He was sitting in the kitchen when his mother came in. He had his uniform on now, the dark green wool of the American storm troopers. Lorea looked away.

"You're up early, Lee Roy," Lorea said, and it was routine, as she had said it would be.

"Do you want some breakfast?" she asked.

"The usual," said Lee Roy. And Lorea went to work.

Lee Roy's father came in, sat down at the head of the table, and opened the *Lubbock Avalanche-Journal*, as always. And they ate breakfast together. They talked about the price of gasoline, about how Jane was doing with her pregnancy. Lorea talked about the Bible study group at the Methodist church, and what readings had been assigned.

Lee Roy understood.

"I have to go to the airport this morning," he said. "Would it be all right if I leave my car here a few days, until Danny comes to pick it up?"

His father looked up from the paper. His eyes were red around their edges this morning.

"It's all right with me," he said. "Is it okay with you, Lorea?"

Lorea said it was.

"I'll need a ride to the airport," said Lee Roy.

The kitchen was quiet for a moment.

"I don't think I can do it," said Lee Roy's father. "I have to work at the station." He was looking at the paper again.

Silence again.

"I can drive you," said Lorea. "You'd better get your things."

The Herron family stood up from the kitchen table. Chair legs slid on the linoleum, dishes clanked, and the counter was wiped. And then it was time.

Lee Roy's father shook his hand and put his arm around him. He did not look at Lee Roy as he turned to go to work.

Lorea had her winter coat on. Lee Roy picked up his valise and followed his mother down the hallway. When he passed his bedroom, he paused and looked inside before moving on.

At the airport, Lorea parked the Fairlane in the short-term lot. "I'm coming in with you," she said.

Carrying his valise in one hand and holding on to the garrison cap of his green winter uniform with the other, Lee Roy walked with his mother across the asphalt lot. It was Christmas and the airport was busy and full of smiles—young people were coming home for the holiday. Lorea took her son's arm.

Inside, at the check-in counter, Lee Roy set his valise on a scale. A young American Airlines employee stared at him. She saw the Marine Corps uniform and a mother standing next to her son, and her face was set—she said nothing. She hoisted the valise onto the conveyor belt, and it disappeared through the hanging rubber slats.

Lee Roy stepped back and faced his mother.

"I wish there was one more thing we needed to do now, Lee Roy, to stretch out the time that we don't have."

Lee Roy nodded.

"But since there isn't," said Lorea, "I'll take your hand, just like when you were a little boy, and I'll walk you toward that gate."

Lee Roy nodded again. They walked a few steps, then they stopped. He hugged his mother.

"You come back to us, now," she said, still holding her arms around him. There were others in the airport check-in area who saw this, but they looked away. The older ones understood, the ones who remembered other wars.

"I'll come back, Mother," said Lee Roy.

And then Lorea turned and walked out the sliding glass doors of the airport, and she did not look back.

Lee Roy stood waiting for a while, watching her until her figure became tiny, and until he could not see her anymore.

There was a mailbox standing by the check-in counter. Lee Roy reached inside the jacket of his uniform and he withdrew an envelope, addressed to his friend Charles Lance. Inside was another letter, one for Charles to deliver to Lee Roy's parents if circumstances made it necessary. The letter read:

November 23d, 1968

Mother and Daddy;

When you read this I'll be dead or missing in action. This letter is my way of saying goodbye and is a final thank you for being such wonderful parents. The love and the respect that I've always had for the two of you is so deep that mere words are inadequate. I'm so terribly sorry to have caused you such grief and sadness.

Please believe me when I say that I have no regrets. I was given the best parents that a child could have. I was taught to love God and our country, and since it was God's will that I die young, I'm proud to die as a Marine defending America.

Please, do not blame anyone for my death and do not be bitter. I have only one thing to ask and that is for the two of you to go to church, to earnestly seek Christ, and to become truly devout Christians. I say this, for I know that I'm going to join Christ in Heaven, and I want you both to be with me and Danny.

Concerning Danny, please help her all you can and when she finds herself another husband, please treat the both of them with kindness and love, and I don't want her to live as a widow.

If it had been God's will that Danny and I were to have children, I only hope that I could have been one half the parent that you, my beloved Mother and Father, were to me.

God bless and keep you.

Your loving son,
Lee Roy

[10]
December 1968
Street without Joy

Lee Roy's journey to Vietnam began that day in an American Airlines two-engine commuter plane from Lubbock to Dallas. People stared at him in the waiting area before he boarded the plane. It was not a good time for young men in uniform. It is hard for young people today to understand that in 1968 many people in the United States blamed the soldiers for a war they considered dumb.

On the plane, a middle-aged woman reexamined her boarding pass, then sat down next to Lee Roy, edged away from him, and turned some so she would neither see him nor touch him.

From Dallas to San Francisco, the Marine Corps had assigned Lee Roy to a larger plane, an American Airlines 707. On this flight, Lee Roy sat in between two Dallas businessmen, both of whom had served as enlisted men in the army during World War II. They asked Lee Roy some about Vietnam and where he would be going, but they soon began to tell their own stories of long ago, war stories. Lee Roy tried to look out the window.

Lee Roy could not see out, but he could feel that he was leaving Texas now, flying at 35,000 feet above the hammered valleys of the Panhandle as they headed north and west. He thought of his third-grade teacher, Miss Terrill, who had retired at the end of the school year. He remembered the punch and cookies, and tablecloths on the long cafeteria tables, something that had seemed strange to him. He had not understood the notion of retirement, of growing older, of change that came with the years, and now he was involved in such a change himself. He wondered what had happened to Miss Terrill. Lee Roy kept his eyes closed during the second half of the flight, mostly so he would not have to talk with the businessmen. But he did not sleep.

In San Francisco it was late afternoon when Lee Roy picked up his valise at the baggage claim area. There was an air force enlisted man waiting for him, and, outside, a gray U.S. Air Force bus. Others were also there boarding, U.S. Army and Marine Corps men, mostly enlisted. As he sat waiting for the trip to Travis Air Force Base, Lee Roy looked out at the flashy women of San Francisco, the short skirts, the long hair. They all seemed to be blond, tall, and slender. Then there were the young men, some with equally long hair, necklaces, and sandals. Lee Roy had to look away from them. He was crossing over into a new universe now, to a time and place where America had taken a stand and men now had to fight for it. The bus started, the driver closed the swinging door. Lee Roy peered out through the windows for one last look.

The trip up the mountains to Travis was slow. The bus rattled and heaved at every curve, as the driver, a junior enlisted man, wandered through great arcs in search of gears. The young enlisted men talked loudly, perhaps to show that they were neither sad nor afraid, but Lee Roy was quiet and mostly looked out his window. As they passed through the Travis main gate, they were routed to the spare rooms of transient quarters, and then lined up in the mess hall for a late dinner. At four the next morning they were awakened. Placed on another bus, they crossed an airfield to the great hangars on the other side. Here they stepped off the bus into the open air. In front of them, in the dark on the tarmac, was a great civilian 707, painted white, with the red logo of Continental Airlines on its side. Each man kept his seabag close. Their names were checked off on a clipboard, they were each handed an orange and a cup of coffee from a large urn, and they stood waiting for dawn. Then they were all sent up into the plane, three seats on each side of the center aisle, no first class, no assigned seats. Nobody talked much.

After what seemed a long time, the great engines whined to life, and the jet began to roll slowly to the far end of a runway. Here the engines ratcheted up, and the plane lurched forward. Lee Roy looked out the window at the outlines of Travis Air Base buildings, at trucks sitting by the runway, at the low, drought-browned California hillsides close by, and quietly to himself said goodbye to America. Then the engines roared, and the plane lifted off toward the dark and uncertain Pacific sky.

The great jet banked quickly to the north, heading for the great circle route over the Pacific that would take them to a U.S. base in Japan. Lee Roy tried to get a look at the city of San Francisco as the plane powered its way to 35,000 feet, but the clouds were low, it was still dark, and little could be seen.

Lee Roy looked at the flight attendants. They appeared old to him, grizzled veterans of the Vietnam War in their own right. When he had flown on commercial flights before, the stewardesses had all seemed so young, so fresh, so beautiful. Here it was as if the plane and its crew had been hardened in the fiery cauldron of their work, ferrying young men to war across the Pacific, ferrying the veterans home, and they had grown old prematurely.

Lee Roy looked about. There was a young man in every seat.

In an era thirty years before civilian airlines would approach efficiency standards for "seat miles flown," the Military Assistance Command in Vietnam had 100 percent utilization of its transports. This 707 had been modified to be a great ferry boat of the sky. Rows of soldiers stretched all the way to the front bulkhead, and all the way to the rear. All were men, and all wore khaki uniforms. Soon enough they would change to dark-green utility uniforms, jungle utilities, and jungle boots that would be issued on Okinawa. The khaki uniforms would wait for them there, unaltered. But will *we* be the same, wondered Lee Roy.

Each young man was alone with his thoughts as the plane climbed high to the north and west. Later, through the long hours of the perpetual morning during the twenty-four-hour flight, Lee Roy looked out the window and he tried to make out the ocean below. Lee Roy decided that he would learn something new each day during his year overseas.

Below was a vast, flat, blue-green ocean surface, stretching in all directions. The plane droned on. Lee Roy dozed and woke. And still there was the Pacific below. It looked calm, peaceful, glinting in the sunlight. How could it represent a place of such violence? Lee Roy wondered about this.

The plane passed slowly over small, snow-shrouded islands, probably the Aleutians, thought Lee Roy. He was next to a window, so he could see white and brown rocky speckles, curving in an arc toward Asia in the blue-green sea.

Lee Roy looked for ships below, but he could not see any. Then, after a time of straining his eyes, squinting into the bright blue Pacific, at midday he thought perhaps he was seeing some: small white specks seven miles below. And after deciding that these specks were ships, he watched them carefully, wondered who was on them and what they were doing so far north in winter.

The flight continued, sunny, timeless, as if floating over the vast sea. Lee Roy kept his eyes closed much of the journey, but he was awake and thinking.

Finally the plane began its gradual descent to the Japanese islands. It was still daylight of the same day. A day had been added to the calendar as they crossed the International Date Line. Lee Roy pondered that one and couldn't quite understand it.

Japan seemed very green and small to Lee Roy as the great jet slowly came down over the northern islands, over Tokyo, toward the Iwakuni airfield. As they flew over Tokyo, the pilot came on the loudspeaker for the first time and announced that they were right about where the Doolittle Raiders had been twenty-six years before, when they had swept in from the aircraft carrier *Hornet* in the eastern sea to bomb the city. How strange it seemed. The Asian wars, then and now.

They landed at the Iwakuni Air Station on December 23. The stewardesses told the soldiers that the day that had been taken away from them during the flight would be given back to them when they returned, although it might have made more sense to consider they'd just had an extra day. Yes, thought Lee Roy. Many things will be given back to us, to me, when I return. He liked thinking of it that way, and he felt ready for what lay ahead. The plane came to rest at the terminal, and its doors were opened.

After a strange day and night of sitting and dozing in transient officers' quarters up the hillside from the airstrip, Lee Roy was back at the Iwakuni terminal building. Now there were fewer men, just the marines from the previous day's flight, standing now in black leather boots and the green utility uniforms of the field. The army troops had left them, to find their own way to Vietnam. From here the marines would be going it alone.

The marines would have a different plane for today's flight to Ryuku Island, Okinawa, a C-130. This was a propeller plane, a field plane: painted field green, with green nylon-web seats, and so much interior noise that earplugs were handed to them by the flight crew as they boarded.

Later in the day, toward nightfall, they landed at the Kadena Air Base on Okinawa. Rain was falling, and there were deep mists about the airfield as the huge plane bounced hard against the runway and rolled to a stop. The marines inside stood up slowly from their halter seats, and trooped in a row to the jump door and its ladder down.

Lee Roy paused in the doorway. The air was wet, warm, and pungent. Lee Roy imagined that he was smelling the odors of Asia itself, inhaling ten thousand years of heat, feudal societies, dense populations, strange trees, rice paddies, and war. Lee Roy felt that he could smell the war, even here in this old Japanese air base. Lee Roy could see old aircraft dugouts along the side of the airfield, where the Japanese had sequestered their Zeroes for the great air battles over the South China Sea. Lee Roy shook his head and climbed down the steel steps to the tarmac.

There were jeeps waiting for them there, jeeps covered in canvas, rambling, swaying, leaking water, and open to the wind as drivers shifted and lurched the vehicles up hairpin roads to the transient camp, Camp Hague, the way station for all marines going to and coming from Vietnam. You had to go through Camp Hague and Kadena.

The jeeps entered the main gate of the camp, and it was Christmas Eve, Lee Roy guessed. He felt so miserable, so lonely and wet, that he went immediately, keys in hand, to the officers' quarters, took off his boots, and climbed into a lower bunk without undressing. He lay there in the dark, rain dripped through an open seam in the plywood roof, water dripped into little puddles on the concrete floor beside him, and Lee Roy did not care.

For five days Lee Roy remained on Okinawa, awaiting C-130 transport south into Vietnam. Five days of rain, leaky roofs, and mess halls serving ground beef and gravy at breakfast, and hamburgers and Jell-O at dinner. He and the others had been issued their jungle uniforms. Each day he stopped at the camp's assignment office, to see if his name was on the list to report back to the airstrip and flight "down south," as the ones who had been before referred to it.

Up the hill from the assignment office was a small white building. Here, at the base of a very high steel radio antenna, were two small cubicles with radiotelephones in them. The marines in Camp Hague, passing to and from the war to the south, could stand in line waiting for their chance at a three-minute call to a phone number far away, in the United States. Lee Roy considered it. The first two days he did not go there, but on the third he waited in line until his turn came, and then he told the operator the number of his home in Lubbock.

The receiver screeched and squawked. Lee Roy heard the operator's mechanical voice.

"Dialing the number, sir," she said. There was loud static.

"Ringing," said the operator. Lee Roy felt a brief surge of panic. He realized that he did not know what time it was in Lubbock. He did not even know what day it was there. He thought of hanging up.

Lee Roy's father answered. "Hello!" he said. He shouted again into the phone: "Hello!"

"Hello, Dad!" Lee Roy launched the words, and they traversed the great curves of the earth like volleys from an electronic battleship. There was clicking on the line and a delay. It felt exceedingly strange.

"Hello!" said his father a third time.

"This is Lee Roy," said Lee Roy. He felt silly after he had said it. His father had tried to say something, but the clicking of the radio transmission had erased his father's words. Lee Roy waited a second.

"I'm on Okinawa!" said Lee Roy, hoping for communication with his family far away.

"Yes," said his father. "I can hear you."

"How are you?" said Lee Roy, but the words were lost in the clicking and the static.

"The station's doing well," said his father.

"The Fairlane's running well," said his father.

Lee Roy said he was fine again.

Then the operator came on, saying time was up. And the line went dead.

Lee Roy sat holding the receiver in his hand, not hanging it up right away, looking at it as if waiting for something he had not received. Then he hung up, stood, and walked out of the cubicle so that the next marine could enter. No more radiotelephone calls home, Lee Roy resolved.

There were marines coming from Vietnam at Camp Hague, as well as ones heading there. The ones coming out looked dirty to Lee Roy. They did not keep their boots polished, even the officers, and they wore green towels around their necks, even though there was no need for that here. They went outside the gates of the camp frequently, into the small, rural Japanese villages across the southern plain of Okinawa, and they came back drunk. They came back with lipstick on their faces. Lee Roy kept away from them.

The next day, December 29, the lieutenant in charge of flight assignments told Lee Roy that he would be going "in country," as he put it, which meant Vietnam.

Lee Roy packed his gear into his seabag early the next morning, and rode with the duty driver from Camp Hague down to the waiting rooms in the Kadena terminal. There was a separate, small room for officers, and Lee Roy was at first the only one in it. There were simple chairs, fluorescent ceiling lights, and not much else. Officers coming out of Vietnam had to wait in these rooms as well, while their orders were checked and endorsed. A first lieutenant entered, sunburned, dusty, his jungle boots bleached khaki from where he had been and what he had done.

"I'm Lee Herron," said Lee Roy.

"John Smith," said the arriving lieutenant, taking Lee Roy's hand. Lieutenant Smith did not sit easily. He seemed restless, pacing the short floor of the room, listening, looking about.

"Have you come from Vietnam?" asked Lee Roy.

"Yeah," said Lieutenant Smith. He wasn't engaging with Lee Roy. He continued his pacing.

"Are you going home?" asked Lee Roy.

"No," said Lieutenant Smith. "To Tokyo."

Lee Roy waited, to see if the lieutenant with the dirty boots would offer anything more, but he did not.

"Why are you going to Tokyo?" asked Lee Roy.

Lieutenant Smith still did not look at Lee Roy. He was shorter than Lee Roy, perhaps five foot nine, and he was thin, wiry. Lee Roy tried to decide if he looked like a combat veteran marine officer should look.

"I took a prisoner," said Lieutenant Smith. "You get an R and R if you bring back a prisoner." He continued pacing. "Five days in Tokyo."

"You should be very proud," said Lee Roy, starting to stand

up, to shake the man's hand. But he sat back down in the aging plastic chair.

"No," said the other lieutenant. "It was a mistake." He paced like a wild animal in a space too small. He showed no humor. He did not smile. He was talking now, war stories.

"Usually I kill them," he said.

Lee Roy sat suddenly straight.

"The best thing is to kill those slant eyes, don't bring 'em back," he said. He wasn't thinking things over. He was flat and matter-of-fact about it. "Too much paperwork if you bring 'em back," he said.

Lee Roy's face and neck turned somewhat red.

"But this guy 'chieu hoi'd,'" continued Lieutenant Smith, talking to the floor as much as to Lee Roy. "And then the little fucker put his arms around my leg, like begging for mercy." And now he did pause, to see if Lee Roy was following the story. He was. "So we were stuck with the little gook," said Lieutenant Smith, sounding irritated. "I couldn't swing the rifle down and shoot him right off my foot," he said defensively. He looked to Lee Roy for affirmation, but Lee Roy just stared. The other lieutenant resumed pacing.

"So when we got back, the colonel said I have to go to Tokyo for five days." He frowned. He had short brown hair, and Lee Roy tried to imagine what he would have looked like, had they been talking on the Texas Tech campus, attending a party or a lecture.

"Have you been to Tokyo?" asked Lieutenant Smith, suddenly anxious. Lee Roy shook his head no.

"I don't have any clothes to wear beyond these," he said, looking down at his sun-worn jungle utilities, creased and stained, a uniform that had been in use days and nights for a considerable time.

Lee Roy could not think of what to say. This wasn't how he had expected it to be.

"I'm sure you'll find something," said Lee Roy. "Some clothes, I mean."

"I don't know what I'm going to do there," said Lieutenant Smith, now looking at Lee Roy almost plaintively. This is the first time Lieutenant Smith has shown any concern, thought Lee Roy.

"What will I do there?" Smith asked Lee Roy, but Lee Roy could think of nothing. He was uncomfortable with all this. He thought he would change the subject. "But you must be proud to be"—Lee Roy was searching for a word other than "heroic"— "so proud to be part of the Marine Corps team," said Lee Roy. He liked the way he had said it.

Lieutenant Smith stopped across from Lee Roy, his jaw open. Lee Roy had a bad feeling about what was coming.

"Are you shitting me?" asked Lieutenant Smith. He was incredulous.

"Are you shitting me?" he said again. "We're getting our asses kicked down there." He was lecturing now. "We land our guys in an LZ out in the middle of a piss pot from nowhere, and we don't know why we're there except the colonel has said 'go there,' and we walk around in circles, and a few guys trip booby traps and get their legs blown off, and then the North Vietnamese ambush one of our squads and knock off three or four men, and we spend the next day or two trying to get their bodies, and we lose two more doing that, and then the choppers come again and we evac out and back to Combat Base Baldy or wherever, and then we get drunk in the plywood O club out there, and we wonder what the fuck we're doing and why we're doing it."

Lee Roy couldn't believe what he had heard. He felt a rush of blood through his head, and he couldn't speak.

"But you can't run away," Lieutenant Smith said intensely, and he approached Lee Roy as he said it. "Do you know why?" he asked.

Lee Roy sat silently.

"Because there's nowhere to go," said Lieutenant Smith. "There's just nowhere to go," and with that he seemed to relax some, to show resignation to things that can't be changed.

"And then we get up and do it all again the next day," he said.

At that point the corporal who managed the boarding of planes opened the door and said, "Lieutenant Herron?"

Lee Roy nodded. He could do nothing more than stand, pick up his seabag, and walk out the door, held open by the corporal.

The flight to Da Nang Air Base lasted about two hours. Lee Roy sat again in a green nylon-web seat, his back against the cold steel frame of the aircraft, his seabag between his legs. Again he sat quietly and thought.

The cumbersome C-130 lumbered south to Da Nang, making a steep descent to minimize terrain overflight. Lee Roy heard later that two Phantom fighters from the 1st Marine Air Wing had risen to accompany the transport plane down. They landed and bumped to a stop on the landing strip, with Monkey Mountain looming over them to the south and Division Ridge above them to the north.

The crew kept the aircraft far out on the runway, stopped at a short, angled pullout on the tarmac. The troops stepped down and quickly climbed into waiting six-by-six trucks that were lined up along the runway. On the other side of the runway was another C-130, broken in two, still burning at its midsection. Lee Roy stared. When the wind turned he could feel the heat of the fire. He had arrived in Vietnam.

"Rockets, sir," said a driver. Lee Roy nodded and swung himself up into the passenger seat while enlisted men climbed into the back.

On Division Ridge, the 1st Marine Division headquarters had been carved out of the hillside, stitched into it with generations of barbed wire, concrete bunkers, and dug-in emplacements for machine guns and howitzers. Lee Roy reported to G-1, the personnel section, in the headquarters building itself. This building, thickly fronted with walls and facings of poured concrete, looked out across the flat plain below, with the South China Sea to the east and the dark blue-green ridge of Monkey Mountain to the south. Lee Roy paused on the steps of the entranceway, looking back, trying to feel the military might of a great nation in this setting and in the scene below. All around there were trucks, jeeps, and marines offloading supplies, opening barbed wire gates, and closing them. And in the distance he could see two Phantoms dropping napalm bombs across a reverse slope of Monkey Mountain. It was very far away, far beyond sound or concussion waves from the strike, but Lee Roy could see the orange sliding flashes of the napalm, like smudges on a child's drawing.

For a moment, Lee Roy puzzled at seeing napalm strikes so close to Division Ridge. After three full years of war, and U.S. dominance of their Asian enemies, these air strikes were close to the headquarters of the 1st Marine Division. What did it mean? Then Lee Roy turned, picked up his seabag, and entered the personnel office.

Inside, in a cave-like room with too-small windows, metal field desks were pushed up against walls, with lance corporals and corporals hard at work on typewriters. In the center of the room was a larger, camouflage-green metal desk, and behind it a captain wearing khakis. The captain wore thick glasses, and his desk was piled erratically with papers that blew and shifted in the cross-breeze of the room's several fans.

Lee Roy laid his orders on the captain's desk, stepped back one step, and stood at attention.

The captain looked down at the face page of the orders, the page stamped "Original," and without looking up said, "You're going to the 3rd Marine Division. This is the 1st. Third is at Dong Ha."

A corporal sitting to the side turned around to see Lee Roy, and said, "You can stay at the temporary officer quarters tonight, sir, over there." And he pointed through many walls and stacked sandbags to the western side of the headquarters complex. "Then you can get on the C-130 to Dong Ha tomorrow morning. Down at the airstrip." There was a pause. Lee Roy stood still, waiting for something more professional, more military, more definitive. But he could see already that it would not come.

"The C-130 don't take reservations over here," added the corporal, and others in the room snickered without looking up from their clerical chores. "All you gotta do is show up at the airstrip tomorrow at eight." There was a pause. "And then wait," said the corporal.

Lee Roy picked up his orders and his seabag, and he walked out the swinging screen door into the sunshine of Da Nang. He turned to the right, and walked down the long façade of division headquarters to a green Quonset hut at the end, which he presumed to be the temporary officers' quarters.

In the TOQ on Division Ridge, Lee Roy lay on a thin mattress above a bare-spring cot during the night of December 29. There was a long row of these cots, musty and dusty witnesses to the passing of many young officers. And what had happened to them, wondered Lee Roy? None were there now but him. He placed his head against his seabag and tried to sleep.

He dozed a while, but bedbugs crawled out of the aged mattress and began tormenting Lee Roy's bare legs. He stood up and threw the mattress to the concrete floor, disgusted. And he no longer felt like sleeping.

Lee Roy walked to the end of the TOQ and stood looking out the screen door. Through the screen he could see the flashing lights of artillery along the plain below Division Ridge, spurting small tongues of flame in the night, and sending their missiles high into the darkness on arcs aimed at other men out there beyond the wire. He could hear the thumping of the cannons, faintly muffled by the distance. Lee Roy mused to himself, as he sometimes had, that the war would be over and all the enemy dead before he could see action. He looked down at the artillery fire, and he looked to the darker mountains beyond, to the west. Something was out there, he thought. But what?

Lee Roy returned to his bunk, lay down on the bare springs, and slept and dreamed uncomfortably. In one dream there were bright lights everywhere, and in the lights a face, floating and strange, came close to him, contorted and grimacing. He tried to reach for the face but he could not move. There was a great commotion about, but there was no sound, and Lee Roy seemed distant from the movements and the activity around him. There was only the face and the lights coming toward him.

Lee Roy was up early on December 30. He hitched a ride with a jeep leaving the headquarters compound, and at the airstrip he found the C-130 revving its engines for the short trip north to the big marine combat base at Dong Ha and the headquarters of the 3rd Marine Division in the field. Lee Roy was getting used to the rhythm of the C-130s. Looking out the window, as the pilot made the typically steep and sudden descent of combat aircraft in Vietnam, Lee Roy could see the Dong Ha base, a large, sandy excavation from the green earth of Quang Tri Province, circled with a road and rows of strung wire. Everywhere there were scars in the ground from bombs and shells of battles past.

The landing strip at Dong Ha was dirt, overlain with steel mesh. They landed hard, and dust flew because it was the dry season, and the season of heat. The pilots turned the aircraft around quickly, as if anxious to reload and leave. When the crew chief wrestled open the forward door, a blast of hot air and dust entered the plane, and Lee Roy closed his eyes. There were six or seven others on the flight from Da Nang, mostly enlisted replacements, and they filed down the steel ladder to the airstrip, holding their gear and seabags slung over one shoulder. Jeeps were waiting for them, and they were taken to the headquarters buildings of the 3rd Marine Division.

In an open jeep, on the short ride, Lee Roy looked at the dirt streets of the Dong Ha Combat Base, stained dark brown by weekly spraying of fuel oil to hold down the dust. Branching off the streets were rows of screened huts with green steel roofs, sandbags holding down edges of the roofs, and sandbags piled against the sides. Electrical wire was strung openly from building to building. And the marines Lee Roy saw on the streets were all armed, carrying M16s or pistols, and each wore a steel helmet and flak jacket.

The headquarters of the 3rd Marine Division was shrouded in dark green paint and plaster over rounded edges of concrete revetments. Entry doors were in defilade, behind turns of concrete, and only the smallest red diamond on the wall at the front of the building hinted at its function. The red three in a diamond casing: the insignia of the marine division that had never come home from World War II, composed of the 9th, 4th, and 3rd infantry regiments.

Lee Roy and the enlisted replacements filed inside the central structure in the headquarters complex. It was cool and dark inside. A staff sergeant escorted the enlisted men to his cubicle down a hallway lit by swinging lightbulbs. A major met Lee Roy, smiled, and grasped his hand. "Welcome to the 3rd Division," said the major. His grip was sure. He seemed to know that Lee Roy was coming. He wore no name tag. "The general wants to see you," said the major. From the look on Lee Roy's face, he thought quickly to add, "Don't worry! Out here the division commander personally meets and greets every new officer."

The major ushered Lee Roy into a larger room, with more overhead lightbulbs and a larger desk with the red diamond of the division on the front. Maj. Gen. Raymond G. Davis stood up from behind the desk and motioned for Lee Roy to take a seat.

It was difficult for Lee Roy to take a seat in front of General Davis. The most highly decorated marine officer on active duty at that time, Davis had every personal medal except the junior enlisted man's Navy Achievement Medal. He had the Navy Cross and Purple Heart from Peleliu in World War II, the Medal of Honor from the Chosin Reservoir fights in Korea, and two Silver Stars and a Bronze Star. It was said of him that his junior officers at his last duty station had tried to figure a way to award him the Navy Achievement Medal so that he would have every personal medal in the Navy Department, but Davis had refused, saying "I didn't earn it." Lee Roy stood in front of one of the greatest Marine Corps heroes.

General Davis came around the field desk behind which he sat, and Lee Roy felt more comfortable sitting down when he saw that General Davis was short. He couldn't have been over five foot six, and Lee Roy towered over him at six foot two. Lee Roy wondered about that. He had heard that Audie Murphy had been short. A brief thought occurred to him that perhaps all the tall heroes had been shot in the head on those days of fire and fury that bore with them the big medals.

General Davis sat down, and Lee Roy felt his heart starting to quicken.

"Welcome to the 3rd Division," said General Davis. He spoke softly, with a mild Georgia accent. He had close-cropped dark hair, with handsome, dark eyebrows. He looked fit, and thin. Lee Roy thought to himself that he couldn't have weighed more than 145 pounds. He couldn't have won the medals in hand-to-hand fighting, thought Lee Roy. He was too small. Then how did he do it? Lee Roy wondered.

"I've been here since May," said General Davis, "and I wanted to be sure I met every newly assigned officer." He paused and looked intently at Lee Roy. Lee Roy didn't know what to do or say. He sat stiffly, not even looking directly at the general.

"The 3rd Division spent too much of its time in 1967 holed up in its combat bases, Mr. Herron," said General Davis. Lee Roy had not been called mister before by a senior officer. He kind of liked it. He had the feeling that he would do anything for this southern gentleman.

"That's not the way we do things, Mr. Herron," continued the general. "That's not the way marines win wars."

Lee Roy was sure he would do absolutely anything for this man. If this man even hinted at something he wanted, Lee Roy would do it. If this man *imagined* something that he wanted Lee Roy to do, he would do it.

"The North Vietnamese 221B and 221A Divisions have had free rein across the western reaches of I Corps since the Tet Offensives and the Khe Sanh fights early this year," said General Davis. He rose and walked to a large map of Quang Tri Province on the wall. He pointed.

"I want the 9th Marines out there," he said, and he pointed with his index finger to the interlocking ridgelines and mountains of northwestern South Vietnam, adjacent to Laos, where the DMZ butted up against the border. "I want the 9th Marines to locate, close with, and destroy the enemy, wherever he may be," said the general. "The 9th Marines have fought many good fights," he said. Then he paused, and in the quiet, clear, sharpness of this small gentleman Lee Roy could now feel a hint of his leadership force, his will and determination. "But I want the 9th Marines out of their combat base there at Vandegrift." He was done referencing the map. General Davis returned to his chair.

"And I want you to help them, Mr. Herron," he said quietly.

Lee Roy suddenly felt his whole world become wavy, as though he was in a great aquatic battlefield.

"I'm sending you out to the 9th Marines," said General Davis. Lee Roy could tell he was nearing the end of his talk. "They'll be going out soon as part of a big operation coming up, Operation Dewey Canyon, and I want you to help them, Mr. Herron."

And then it was over. General Davis stood up. Lee Roy stood up. Lee Roy couldn't help himself. He saluted. Even though he held his utility cover in his left hand, along with the orders and records, he saluted.

General Davis went back behind the desk to his papers. "Do not salute uncovered, Mr. Herron," he said without looking up.

Later that afternoon Lee Roy was dropped off by the same jeep and driver at the Dong Ha airstrip, where a CH-46 helicopter was revving up for the trip to Vandegrift Combat Base, the headquarters of the 9th Marine regiment to the west. The windows were open along the sides of the helicopter, and the crew was shirtless, swiveling the M60 machine guns about at each mid-fuselage window. The crew chief, with a large steel helmet almost obscuring his face, leaned out the window.

"Better stand aside, lieutenant!" he yelled against the wind and the noise of the great twirling blades above. Lee Roy stepped back, into the tail shadow of the machine.

Suddenly both machine guns fired, blasting and rocking the helicopter, and Lee Roy dropped everything and clapped his hands against his ears. The M60s fired out over the wire along the narrow sides of the landing strip, scorching the air with cordite and tracers. Lee Roy stood, still holding his hands over his ears. The crew chief leaned out the side windows again, and yelled back at him: "Okay now, lieutenant! We have to test 'em before every flight! Gooners everywhere!"

Lee Roy climbed into the helicopter through the open tail door. He sat down on one of the web seats along the hull and buckled himself in.

The ride to Vandegrift was wild. The CH-46 flew low, just above treetops, and it ducked and curved along the contours of the landscape, tilting to forty-five-degree angles as it sliced its way up and down low valleys, and rearing its nose suddenly up and then down over ridgelines and crests. Lee Roy felt like he was going to vomit. The crew chief sat opposite him, smiling and mumbling into his radio mouthpiece the whole way. Two PFCs held onto the receiver assemblies of the machine guns, blasting away from time to time at nothing Lee Roy could see in the thick jungle below. One of them yelled at the top of his lungs, so loud that even in the din of the roaring helicopter engines he could be heard: "Fuck that!" The combat base came upon them so fast, and the pilot landed so hard in a dusty open area in the center, that Lee Roy thought for a moment they had crashed.

While a Marine Corps jeep cruises by, and prior to the beginning of Operation Dewey Canyon, Marines form a parade unit at Vandegrift Combat Base in Vietnam, temporary home of the 9th Marines, 3rd Marine Division. Courtesy of Norval "Tex" Thomas.

In early 1969, Vandegrift Combat Base was attacked by enemy rocket and mortar fire. This photo from the base was taken by 1st Lt. Norval "Tex" Thomas, a marine who was commissioned with David Nelson and Lee Roy Herron on June 7, 1967. Courtesy of Norval "Tex" Thomas.

"Here we are, sir!" yelled the crew chief. He jerked down a lever at the front of the hull, and the rear platform door descended.

Lee Roy walked out into the sunlit stage of Vandegrift Combat Base, home to the 9th Marine Regiment in Quang Tri Province. The Walking Dead, they were called.

From what Lee Roy could see, Vandegrift was not much more than a field emplacement, with tents scattered about, the odor of diesel oil and latrines everywhere. And the heat there struck Lee Roy in the chest and staggered him, made him doubt that he could endure it long term. The heat was a killer.

"Over there," yelled the crew chief, though the noise of the helicopter blades had dropped. He pointed to a large, broad tent with plywood sides. "The CP!" he shouted.

Lee Roy carried his seabag over to the CP—the command post of the 9th Marines. He tried not to look awkward in his polished boots and clean uniform, but there was no way around it. He didn't look or act like the other marines there. Lee Roy was "new in country," NIC.

Lee Roy entered the first of the several CP tent buildings that he came upon. Everything inside was plywood and tarred canvas, dust and heat. Colonel Barrow, in command of the 9th Marines, was out, so the executive officer, a major, greeted Lee Roy and brought the personnel NCO over to take Lee Roy's orders, health records, and other papers. One of the supply sergeants came in, and the major asked him to take Lee Roy around, issue him his 782 gear, flak jacket, helmet, and .45 caliber pistol.

"Won't I need an M16?" asked Lee Roy, as he stood up to go with the supply sergeant.

"No," said the major. "We have you assigned to Headquarters and Service Company, with us here at Vandegrift. You won't be going out."

Lee Roy stopped short.

"No!" he said, shocking himself.

"What do you mean, 'no'?" asked the major stiffly.

Lee Roy thought of General Davis.

"I have to go to the field. With the letter companies," said Lee Roy.

For a second, the major could not think what to say.

"You've been to language school," said the major. "You're quite senior as a first lieutenant," he continued. "Almost a captain." He was trying to find the right words here, to be tactful yet direct. "You wear glasses, and marksmanship is not your strength," he said. "There's a war going on out there." He stopped. He could tell by the look on Lee Roy's face that he had said more than enough to mortify him. The major tried to make it better.

"Colonel Barrow thought you would really help us here, in the H&S Company, where we are. You could translate the gook papers we bring in. You could interrogate the prisoners." Lee Roy thought of Lieutenant Smith, now probably wandering about in Tokyo, wearing a PX T-shirt, blue jeans, and jungle boots.

The major softened. "Colonel Barrow returns in a couple of days. Let me discuss this with him. I'll let you know."

[11]
January 1969
The Walking Dead

I knew nothing about what Lee Roy was going through as 1969 began. I had started the roofing job just before Christmas, as Martie had suggested, so I couldn't stay long in Temple. On January 2, law school began again, and Martie resumed her teaching. I don't remember much else about that time. I had no idea what was happening with Lee Roy, and I didn't think about him much.

New Year's Day 1969
Vandegrift Combat Base

Lee Roy spent the last day of 1968 lying and sitting on his cot in a green plywood hooch with screen doors that banged hard when they closed. There were two cots in the hooch; another first lieutenant lived there, but Lee Roy didn't see him much. Above the other lieutenant's cot a .45 caliber "grease gun"—an M3 submachine gun—hung mounted on two nails, with one nail protruding through the trigger guard. The short and ugly muzzle of the weapon was pointed generally toward Lee Roy's cot. After staring at it for a time that morning, Lee Roy rose, walked to the other bunk, took the grease gun from its nails, and examined it. He held it away from himself, carefully, and kept the muzzle pointed at the floor. The gun was heavy and cold. Gingerly, Lee Roy slowly touched his index finger to the trigger, held it there a moment, and then he lifted the gun and placed it back on the nails, pointing it away from his own bunk.

Later that day Lee Roy's roommate returned. The screen door of the hooch creaked open, then clanged shut. Standing in front of Lee Roy was a stocky marine officer, his features dark against a very faded utility uniform.

The officer scowled and his face darkened even more when he saw that Lee Roy was there.

"Fitzpatrick's my name," he said. He did walk over to where Lee Roy sat on his cot. The plywood floor creaked with every step of his boots, and small wafts of dust rose around the footfalls. Lee Roy stood and offered his hand. Lieutenant Fitzpatrick took it.

"Lee Herron," said Lee Roy.

"I'm not Irish," said Lieutenant Fitzpatrick. "I was adopted and the family had an Irish name, but what I am I really don't know." He took Lee Roy's hand and gripped it hard, squeezing more than shaking it. He looked straight into Lee Roy's eyes. There was intensity about this brief encounter that Lee Roy tried to understand. It felt intense, not warm, not engaging.

Indeed, Fitzpatrick did not look Irish. He was short and dark, quick in his movements and in his speech. Lee Roy could not think of anything to say. Fitzpatrick let go of Lee Roy's hand, walked back to his cot, and rummaged in his seabag, which lay on the floor.

"I've got perimeter guard," he said. He did not look again at Lee Roy. He found what he was looking for in the seabag, stood up, and looked at his cot. Noticing that the grease gun was pointing a different direction, Lieutenant Fitzpatrick stepped forward, roughly jerked the gun off its nails, turned it around so that it aimed in the direction of Lee Roy's cot again, and then replaced it on the nails.

Fitzpatrick walked out of the hooch and did not look back. The screen door slammed behind him.

Lee Roy sat still on his cot for a while. Then he stood, walked to the head of Fitzpatrick's cot, and turned the grease gun so that it pointed away again.

He spent the next several days sitting in the hooch, going to the small mess hall for meals, and walking about the perimeter of the base and along the edges of the landing strip. There was the constant sound of gunfire. Lee Roy noticed that the most. Every hour of the day and night: gunfire in the distance. Sometimes the rattling of the fire was close and loud, and Lee Roy would crouch down and wonder. But the other marines seemed to pay no attention to it. Somehow they had become inured to the constant barking of guns, and they had developed an unconscious sense for what was important gunfire and what was background noise.

Lee Roy was waiting for something to change with regard to his assignment, but nothing was happening. Everyone at Vandegrift seemed busy, purposeful, except for him. On about January 5, Lee Roy returned to the regimental command post.

The major who had greeted Lee Roy at his arrival on December 30 stood in the operations room of the CP, in front of a large topographical map. The green and white map, checkered with thousand-meter squares, had the Vandegrift landing strip in its center, and all about its eastern edges were crayon markings of company emplacements, roads and trails, and landing zones.

"Ah, Lieutenant Herron," said the major, without looking over his shoulder at Lee Roy. "You can see our area of operations here.

"We've got 1st Battalion here," he said, pointing to the western edge of Vandegrift.

"We've got 2nd Battalion here, with the artillery," he said, pointing to the eastern edge of Vandegrift.

"And we've got 3rd Battalion here, back towards Dong Ha," he said, pointing up at the northeastern edge of the map.

The major seemed to enjoy the map, pointing to the dots and crayon lines, representing thousands of marines emplaced and wired in. The major reached forward and rubbed off a small area of crayon marking along the edge of 2nd Battalion's position, making it neater.

Lee Roy looked at the western half of the map; in this area there was a long, angled ridgeline, sweeping down to the southwest corner of the map, dividing the area above it and below it into two broad and irregular valleys. Crayon marks were absent in this area.

"What's out here?" asked Lee Roy, and he stepped forward and drew his finger along the ridgeline and the edges of the valleys.

The major hesitated.

"Indian country," said the major. "That's Indian country." He spoke more softly as he said this. For a moment, Lee Roy saw an image in his mind's eye of Comanches riding across the West Texas plains, drawing arrows from quivers, and riding up alongside buffaloes. But then he looked again at the situation map in the combat center, at its contour lines of hills and valleys, and at the Asian names of rivers and other features. The Comanche image didn't fit.

"Indians?" asked Lee Roy.

"Well," said the major, "do you know how we could get a map of, say, southern Nevada, and we could look at all the landmarks, and then we could get into our cars or our jeeps or whatever, and we could go out there to whatever spot we wanted and explore it?"

"Yes," said Lee Roy.

"Well, it's not like that here. We can't go out into those areas," he said, and he drew his hand in a wide arc across large areas of the 9th Marines' operating area.

"Do you mean," Lee Roy stammered, he couldn't help it, "do you mean we're—not winning the war there?"

It sounded terrible to Lee Roy, the way he had said it, and he saw instantly in the frown of the major's face that he had not said it right.

"Well, let's just say that you're going to find out, Lieutenant," said the major. The words had an icy edge to them. "Because that's where you're going."

He stepped forward and drew his finger along the line of the valley below the ridgeline near where they were at Vandegrift, down to the southwest corner of the map.

"You've been assigned to One Nine," said the major. "Alpha Company. Later this month, they'll be going down that ridgeline into the A Shau Valley."

Lee Roy said nothing. He was trying to understand.

"And Colonel Barrow says you're going with them."

January 20, 1969
Alpha Company, 1st Battalion, 9th Marines

At dawn, when light from the east spread rosy fingers into the sky, the CH-46 helicopter supporting Alpha Company, 1st Battalion, 9th Marines, banked sharply down onto the hilltop emplacements of previously abandoned Fire Support Base Shiloh, in the Da Krong Valley, about ten thousand meters south and west of Vandegrift. The crew chief pancaked the rear door of the helicopter and the marine occupants emerged. First Lieutenant Lee Roy Herron, executive officer of Alpha Company, stepped out first into the warm morning air of the base. A heavily armed and pack-laden squad followed. The pilot of the CH-46 did not even slow its rotor blades, only feathered them while the marines exited so that he could lift off immediately after they were out. As the last marine stepped off the steel square of the door, the crew chief cranked the hydraulic lift, the pilot gunned the two interdigitating blades of the CH-46, and the great machine roared off into the brightening day, leaving swirling dust and silence on the hilltop.

Lee Roy looked about at the shredded hilltop they called Fire Support Base Shiloh. The marines who had landed just ahead of him were already turning this spot into a combat-ready base. Lee Roy knew that two 105mm howitzers were due in shortly with the artillery unit, and Alpha Company had to be prepared to secure and defend these big guns, along with the rest of the base.

It seemed to Lee Roy that with each aircraft ride from Lubbock he had moved further and further from the world of rules and reason, and now in this desolate place he had reached the edge of everything he had known. He looked at the dark hills to the west, and noticed the silence compared to the constant rumble of gunfire at Vandegrift. Lee Roy guessed that this would be his first lesson in the bush—that when one heard gunfire here at Fire Support Base Shiloh it would have an entirely different meaning.

A young lance corporal walked up to Lee Roy from the center of the open area on the top of the hill. He had "Boland" stitched on a name tag above the left pocket of his jungle utilities. He did not salute.

"Hello, sir. I'm Lance Corporal Boland. I was told that you probably would want to find the command post and CO as soon as you arrived."

Lee Roy, weighed down by sixty pounds of ammunition, water, C rations, and other gear in his pack, stood facing the lance corporal. He looked down at the M16 in his hand and reminded himself who he was.

"Lieutenant Herron, Lance Corporal," said Lee Roy. The words came out surprisingly warm and confident. Even to Lee Roy. "Yes, I do want to speak to Lieutenant Fox before Captain Barnum's artillery battery arrives from Vandegrift, which is any minute now. Can you take me to Lieutenant Fox?' As Lee Roy spoke, the distant chop of whirring blades could be heard.

"Yes, sir," said Chuck Boland, a young man who would remember Lee Roy for the rest of his life. Boland was eager to move, to have something special to do. They set off to locate Lieutenant Fox at the command post.

It was customary for the executive officer's helicopter to be the last to arrive, and on this day the helicopters carrying Alpha Company all arrived within a thirty-minute period. Lee Roy was pleased that even though he was in the last troop chopper, he did not have to wait long to be on the front lines; he was anxious to take an active role with the troops.

Earlier helicopters had brought 1st Platoon, under the command of 2nd Lt. George Malone; 2nd Platoon, under the command of 2nd Lt. James Davis; and 3rd Platoon, under the command of 2nd Lt. Bill Christman. All were just out of The Basic School, thought Lee Roy.

The commander of Alpha Company, 1st Lt. Wesley Fox, had

arrived on the second chopper from Vandegrift during the fast and efficient airlift. Lee Roy was anxious to find him to see what tasks he could help with that day. He couldn't help but salute when he finally located Fox in the dusty heat of that hilltop emplacement.

"No need to salute out here, Lee," said Lieutenant Fox, already looking past Lee Roy at the emplacements, the cuts and draws around the edges of the hilltop, and the ridgeline networks to the northeast and southwest.

"Let's walk this perimeter, Lee. Come with me," said Fox, already moving out with the company gunnery sergeant walking on his left. Lee Roy followed.

Lieutenant Fox was a "mustang" officer—a former enlisted man who had been promoted. He had been wounded in Korea, and was on his second Vietnam tour. Lee Roy stayed close and tried to learn from him.

They went to each platoon area along the edges of the base. Fox talked with the platoon commanders. The gunnery sergeant talked with enlisted men. Lee Roy listened.

At the western edge of the position, Fox stood exposed on a small promontory, some open high ground facing southwest and the A Shau Valley. He stood away from the group, looking far into the distance, feeling the wind, and looking for something out there that he could not see. Lee Roy stayed close to him. At one point Lieutenant Fox closed his eyes, seeming to listen to the stories of the wind.

"Do you know what that is out there, Lee?" asked Fox, not turning around to look at him. Lee Roy liked it that Fox called him by his first name. It made him feel that Fox was teaching him.

"No, sir," said Lee Roy.

"That's Laos," said Fox, and there was heaviness, determination in his voice.

"The Yellow Brick Road is out there, Lee," said Fox. "We're looking at the Yellow Brick Road."

"Sir?" asked Lee Roy.

"The Ho Chi Minh Trail. That's it out there in those dark valleys you can see to the southwest," and Lieutenant Fox swept his hand across the distant green rows of hills and valleys that angled away from them.

"That's the gook highway out there, where they come into Vietnam from Laos, and where they bring their equipment and supplies."

Everyone in the company command group stared out to where Fox had pointed.

"And when Colonel Barrow gives the word, that's where we'll be going."

The small group of young men stood gazing at dark mountains and shifting mists floating low across the valley depths.

Lee Roy's first Sunday in the bush came on January 26. Alpha Company remained in place at Shiloh. There had been no contacts. No gunfire. Lee Roy went to the command post at about 7:00 a.m.

"Excuse me, Lieutenant Fox," said Lee Roy in a slightly hesitant voice. Fox was sitting down and busy going over detailed maps of Da Krong Valley and A Shau Valley.

"Hello, Lee," he said. He set the maps down. He smiled and looked up.

"I want you to know," said Lieutenant Fox, "that I really appreciate the way you check the lines for me at night. That helps me a lot. And the men appreciate it, too."

Lee Roy started to answer, but Fox wanted to talk.

"I don't have the energy I used to have, and it helps me that you check the lines at night."

Lee Roy didn't think the Marine Corps had "thank you" in its field manuals, so he said nothing.

"You know, Lee, I've been in many campaigns for this man's Marine Corps." When Fox was in a good mood he referred to the Corps as "this man's Marine Corps." Lee Roy didn't understand why.

"I bet I've been in combat more years than you've been in the Marine Corps!" said Lieutenant Fox, and his eyes twinkled; he was pleased with himself.

Lee Roy waited.

"But I've never had a command like this one. These boys are good," he said. "The officers are good. The 9th Marines are going to do something now. They're going to make a difference in this war." He became more intense. He looked directly at Lee Roy.

"The entire 812th Regiment of the North Vietnamese Army is out there, Lee. We just don't know exactly where, but we have a pretty good idea.

"I'd go anywhere with this company, Lee," said Lieutenant Fox, very intense now. "Anywhere. I'd go up against anybody with Alpha Company."

"Yes, sir," said Lee Roy. Lieutenant Fox stopped talking, realizing that Lee Roy had come to see him about something. "But what's on your mind?" he asked.

"Would it be all right if I went to church today?" asked Lee Roy.

Lieutenant Fox stared a moment, as if he had not heard correctly.

"Oh, I know we don't have a real church," explained Lee Roy, "but I hear there's a chaplain over at Fire Support Base Razor, and the helicopters go back and forth, and it's quiet now." Fox was listening. "So I thought if a supply helicopter comes in soon I might hitch a ride over to Razor, and be back by noon?"

Lieutenant Fox seemed relieved.

"Do you see this Bible?" asked Lee Roy, and he pulled the book from a deep side pocket of his uniform. "My parents gave it to me when I graduated from high school in 1963."

Lieutenant Fox looked at the Bible.

"Where are you from, Lee?" Fox asked.

"Lubbock, Texas, sir," answered Lee Roy.

"Well," said Fox, "I guess I'll remember that." He looked again at the Bible that Lee Roy held. "And I guess I'll remember that Bible," he said, and he laughed a little.

"Sure, Lee," said Lieutenant Fox. "You can go to the church service. We'll need the help of God out here before we're done, and the men will need it, too." He turned silent again, as if remembering many things.

"I myself could never—I mean, I just never felt the hand of God much in the way things happened sometimes. I just never could feel it, Lee. But you go ahead."

So when the resupply helicopter stopped at Shiloh less than an hour later, Lee Roy asked if the pilot could drop him at Razor, about ten thousand meters ("ten clicks") south and west of Shiloh, and the pilot agreed.

Salvatore Rubino, navy chaplain to the 9th Marine Regiment, prepared his Sunday service at Fire Support Base Razor, using a stack of C ration boxes and ammo boxes as a pulpit, and more C ration boxes as the pews. The marines who had come for the nine o'clock service sat with heads bowed, and they repeated the Lord's Prayer with Lieutenant Rubino. He read to them from the Bible. He offered them communion, using some of the dry crackers from the C ration boxes. He was light on the sermon, and there was no need of an offering. A Marine Corps photographer, Pfc. C. E. Sickler, Jr., was at Razor that day, and he took a photograph that became widely known after it appeared on the cover of the *Navy Times* on March 5. By that time, Lee Roy would be dead.

Through the first week in February the 9th Marines continued to reinforce their fire support bases on the hilltops in western

On Sunday, January 26, 1969, Chaplain Salvatore Rubino conducts a service at Fire Support Base Razor, as a helicopter unloads ammunition in the background. Lee Roy Herron (right foreground, wearing glasses) thanked Chaplain Rubino afterward for "bringing God to such an ungodly place." Official U.S. Marine Corps photo.

Quang Tri Province, until the three battalions in the regiment were in position to move out into the valleys toward Laos. The operation would be a massive sweep, aimed at finding the NVA 812th Regiment, or other elements of the North Vietnamese Army's Fourth Front that were believed to be out there. The operation would be called Dewey Canyon. The rains had begun, however, and the marines remained in their positions waiting for a break in the weather.

Two Sundays later, February 9, one of the lance corporals in Alpha Company, Lenny Cosner, was shaken awake in his tent by one of his friends.

"Get up, Lenny," his friend said. "There's gonna be a church service."

Cosner groaned. He had had guard duty on the perimeter until midnight, and had been deeply asleep.

"I'm an atheist," said Lenny to the man who had awakened him.

"Get your butt up and get over there. Lieutenant Herron is going to do the service. It might improve your morals to go."

Cosner sat up. He pulled on his boots and rolled himself out of the shelter so that he could see the church service gathering in a huge B-52 bomb crater just down the hill from the company CP. There were many marines there, and Lieutenant Herron had made a cross from engineer stakes, with the help of 3rd Platoon. Lenny walked over and took a seat on the wet ground in the back of the crater.

An enlisted man from another platoon was speaking. Lee Roy stood to the side, next to the cross.

"You have to be ready!" intoned the enlisted man. He was tall, and his voice was deep and it carried well. "You have to be ready to meet your Lord!"

Lenny was not so sure about this kind of sermon. His RTD (rotation tour date) was February 28. He would be going home that day, and he was not planning to meet his maker before then.

"Christ is a choice!" continued the speaker. "You have to make that choice before you're called!" he said. "You cannot wait until that day that the Lord calls your name!"

Lenny did not listen to much more. There were at least seventy-five marines there—over half the company. Lieutenant Herron was speaking now.

"Look to the left, and look to the right!" said Lee Roy. "Look at the man sitting next to you, on your right or on your left!" Most of them did look.

"Some of those men on your right and on your left will not be there in six months. Do not wait for that day!" said Lee Roy. "Surrender yourself to Christ now!"

Lenny Cosner did not like this sermon. He wheeled himself up and over the edge of the crater and returned to his shelter.

Monday, February 10

Lee Roy was up at night at Shiloh, checking the lines and the positions, partly so that Lieutenant Fox and the platoon commanders could get some rest, some relief from their command duties. The executive officer, Lee Roy figured, was the only one who didn't have fixed command responsibilities in Alpha Company, and he was determined to make a difference for the unit as best he could.

"Hi, Lieutenant," said one of the enlisted men in a two-man foxhole on the night of February 10.

"How's it going?" asked Lee Roy, sitting down on the edge of the position, and rotating himself down into it so that he stood with the two marines there and saw things as they saw them.

"Quiet, sir," said the enlisted man.

Lee Roy could not see the man's face in the darkness, only his soft voice. Out here, on the edge of American power and control in the world, everything was quiet in the night. It was not like Vandegrift, thought Lee Roy. This was real out here, he thought. Noises were real out here.

"Is there any movement? Do you hear anything?" asked Lee Roy.

They were on the western edge of the company position, looking out into the ridges and valleys of the A Shau and the Da Krong below them. This was 2nd Platoon's area, 2nd Lt. Jim Davis commanding. Davis was back about a hundred yards from the lines, resting under a shelter strung on wire over a hole. The platoon commanders understood that from midnight on Lee Roy would be checking.

"Nothing, sir," spoke the enlisted man.

Lee Roy looked out into the darkness. He could feel a warm breeze, and there were strange smells, of rain and jungle.

"What's your name?" asked Lee Roy.

"Stoppiello," answered the enlisted man. "Lance Corporal Frank Stoppiello, from 2nd Platoon," he said.

In the dark, Lee Roy tried to look into the face of this young man. Something seemed familiar about him. Something he could not place. He had seen that face before, he thought, and then he moved that thought out of mind.

Stoppiello had a positive way about him. Even here, in a rude hole dug by hand from the reddened earth of the jungle, this young man was eager, proud, and ready.

"How old are you, Lance Corporal Stoppiello?" asked Lee Roy.

Before Stoppiello could answer, a distant hissing came from the sky and glided down gently near them, and then a great clap of thunder erupted from the next emplacement to the north from where Lee Roy and Stoppiello were talking.

There were screams, a terrible sound of rocks and dirt scrabbling down, large pieces of earth torn and flung into the sky, and the deadly whirring sound of shrapnel razors slicing through the air.

And there were more screams.

Lee Roy stood still in Stoppiello's hole. He knew he was supposed to get up and go to the place where the shell had hit, but he was still for a moment, not wanting to go.

"Let's go, Lieutenant!" said Stoppiello, and Stoppiello was up and out of the hole and headed to where the impact had been, and Lee Roy was going with him. Others were moving to the site to check on the damage.

When Lee Roy came on the scene, Lieutenant Davis and his platoon sergeant were already there. There were bodies there, hard to distinguish from other objects on the ground at first. Lee Roy knew that they were there, and he did not want to look, but he looked.

One body lay broken and unmoving, like a rag doll draped across the edge of the four-man gun emplacement. The man lay face down, Lee Roy could see, and Lee Roy did not want to see him rolled over.

Another man lay on his back, against the side of the position, away from where the shell had hit. He had been blown open—split from his crotch to his neck—and the two halves of his body were spread out from each other. His face was there, looking up into the night sky, but Lee Roy did not look at the face.

A third man had been at the edge of the emplacement next to the shell impact, and the top half of him, severed completely at the waist, lay plastered into the rough edges of the shell crater.

The fourth man was alive. Lee Roy knelt down beside him, and he took Lee Roy's hands. He was euphoric and babbling.

"Oh, Lieutenant, I'm alive! I'm alive!" Lee Roy held his hands. "Thank God! Thank God! I'm alive!"

"Praise God," said Lee Roy. "We must praise God."

"Yes," said the wounded marine. "Yes! And yes! And yes!"

And then the corpsmen were there, and they took charge of the scene, and Lee Roy stood up and backed away from it all. Lieutenant Davis came up beside him.

"Friendly fire," said Davis. His words were hard and bitter. The two lieutenants stood there, side by side above the shell crater.

"That one was supposed to be on R&R in Hawaii with his wife," said Davis, and he pointed to the man split in two. "But we couldn't get him out. And that one was supposed to go home in a month." He pointed to the one lying face down, quiet in the earth.

"That one," said Davis and he pointed to the man cut in half, "you know, I'm not sure who he is." He paused. "Or was."

Lieutenant Davis turned and walked to his other positions, and Lee Roy looked again at the scene and tried to understand it all.

[12]
February 1969
At the Iron Gate

At dawn on February 11, Operation Dewey Canyon began.

Alpha Company spent the day airlifting to Fire Support Base Erskine, about twenty thousand meters south and west from Shiloh. The entire 1st Battalion, 9th Marines (1/9), was assembling here, where everything beyond Erskine was Indian Country.

As with his journey to Shiloh, Lee Roy rode with the troops on a CH-46 chopper into Erskine. He was anxious to see what this fire support base so close to the enemy would be like. As the helicopter swept down in a near vertical descent, it tilted to its starboard side, and Lee Roy, looking down, could see a CH-47 helicopter on its side, burning in the draw just short of the landing zone. Oily smoke from the burning aviation gasoline rose up, shrouding the area.

Alpha Company arrived in another efficient airlift, and, after disembarking, the marines prepared for a brief stay at Erskine. New men had joined Alpha previously at Vandegrift, and they had been parceled out into the rifle platoons as they joined the company. Alpha Company now had 180 marines, 60mm mortars, and M79 grenade launchers, along with ammunition, C rations, and water. The company was prepared and in its attack phase.

The next morning, Alpha Company moved out, marching across the wire and down the hillside in a long green column, rifles and helmets clanking, jungle boots cutting into the red earth with sharp treads. As Lee Roy prepared to step over the wire he thought about how proud he was to be going into battle with his fellow marines. This was the experience he had wanted ever since he was a young boy.

But Lee Roy's exhilaration was tempered by the actions of the battalion chaplain. As 1/9 crossed the line of departure (LOD) into A Shau Valley, Lee Roy passed the battalion chaplain who was walking to the Helicopter Landing Zone (HLZ) to catch the next bird out. He had told his battalion commander that he could not continue with the operation, that he was overcome by heat.

During Alpha Company's movements, Lee Roy always brought up the rear, while Lieutenant Fox was in the lead. Although Lieutenant Fox was not with Lee Roy as they passed the chaplain, Fox knew that it would hit Lee Roy hard to see the man of cloth quit the battalion. The 1st Battalion, 9th Marines, went on the attack without their official chaplain, but Lee Roy assumed the responsibility on his own and went above and beyond the call of duty to organize and hold spiritual meetings. He assured that counseling was available to all marines who wanted it. During the next eleven days, Lee Roy took the place of the battalion chaplain and was spiritually involved with his fellow marines during this critical and stressful time.

The battalion attacked south from Erskine, across the Da Krong and into A Shau Valley. This was NVA Base Camp Area 611. Route 922 entered this valley from Laos to the west. Alpha Company and Charlie Company moved down one ridgeline, with Bravo Company and Delta Company moving down another; together they searched the valleys in between. The jungle was thick here, daytime temperatures were in the nineties, and it was humid.

Now there were signs of the enemy: base camps with cleared areas and gun emplacements, abandoned in the opening moves of the chess game for human lives that had been named Operation Dewey Canyon. There were camouflaged roads, with trees sawed down mid-trunk and then set up to hide the open space from the air. And here and there was the detritus of war, empty ammunition cans, wrappers, and latrines. The marines moved more quietly now, in staggered columns along the natural seams of the earth and the jungle, a ridgeline, a streambed. The enemy was close now. Lee Roy saw the signs, and he wondered why they had pulled back.

And there was contact. Alpha Company moved slowly, one platoon in front, the other two hanging back, probing the flanks, staying close. There was firing, and men on the edges were hit. The marines blasted back into the surrounding jungle, and they retrieved their dead and wounded, and searched for open areas for medevac helicopters to land.

During these days in February the company lost four wounded and one killed. The battalion operations officer, Major Donald Kennon, was killed on February 13. There were heat casualties who had to be evacuated each day. Progress was slow.

Lee Roy wrote his last letter home on February 18, to Charles Lance. In the letter he said that Alpha Company was in a "rock 'em sock 'em" war, and suffering casualties. Lee Roy wrote that he was becoming a veteran, learning the ways of warfare in the jungle. He asked Charles not to show the letter to his family.

On the evening of February 19, after darkness fell, vehicle sounds were heard coming from the west and south, the direction of Laos. The men listened to the diesel engines and clanking of steel. There was quiet talk. Tanks were feared. The NVA had overrun a Special Forces camp with tanks near Khe Sanh the previous year.

The next morning, Charlie Company, in the battalion lead, discovered two abandoned 122mm field guns on the ridgeline. Charlie Company stayed with the guns, and Alpha Company passed through and moved on toward the Laotian border where the NVA were believed to be improving route 922.

On February 20, Alpha Company took Lang Ha-Bn, on the Laotian border. Bunkers and ammo sheds were found, as well as an antiaircraft gun.

That evening the NVA fired mortars at Alpha Company.

The next day, 1st Platoon moved down the west side of the ridgeline to A Shau Valley. A hospital complex of bunkers and caves was found and destroyed.

At midday, the battalion asked for a platoon-sized sweep of the valley to the east, having picked up intelligence that a sizable force might be collecting there to recapture the 122mm guns. Lieutenant Christman with 3rd Platoon was sent into the valley to the east. The 3rd Platoon became heavily engaged with an NVA force, and Alpha Company was ordered to withdraw back up the ridgeline. That night 3rd Platoon moved back up to rejoin Alpha Company.

Lt. Col. George W. Smith, the battalion commander, ordered Alpha Company to return to the valley the next morning to eliminate the threat. Artillery fire pockmarked the valley during the night. Lieutenant Fox met with his officers.

"Can you find the North Vietnamese position again, Bill, where you were in contact today?" Lieutenant Fox asked Lieutenant Christman.

Christman was sitting on the ground, his back against a tree.

He spoke slowly. "Yes," he said. "I can find 'em." He paused. "But I'm not sure I want to find those guys again. There were a lot of them. And they weren't running."

"Most likely they've moved off by now," said one of the other lieutenants. "They don't stick around and wait."

Lieutenant Fox looked at his officers. There was Christman, commanding 3rd Platoon; Jim Davis with 2nd; Malone with 1st; and Lee Roy, the executive officer.

"Right," said Fox. "I don't expect they'll be there." The officers all looked at him. Only Lee Roy stood. The others sat on the ground, holding their steel helmets or sitting on them. There had been no water resupply for three days, and none of them had shaved. They had not changed their jungle utility uniforms, nor would they for the entire operation.

"What if they are still there?" asked Christman. Fox looked at him.

"Check your men," he said. "Two-man watches out in front all night. We'll move out down into the valley at first light."

And so it was. The young men returned to their platoons. Lee Roy stayed with Lieutenant Fox.

That night, Lee Roy sat against a tree, near Lieutenant Fox, the company gunnery sergeant, and two or three more junior enlisted men with the command group. As others slept, Lee Roy sat looking at the sky, trying to find the stars that would guide him at dawn. The dawn of February 22, Lee Roy's last day.

In the early morning light, Lieutenant Fox lined the platoons up, with 2nd Platoon in the lead, 1st just behind, and 3rd in the rear. Lee Roy also moved to the rear, to be in position to move forward and take over if needed. Fox assigned Lieutenant Christman to accompany Lieutenant Davis with the 2nd Platoon, to serve as a guide for Alpha Company to take the forks in the trail that would lead to the NVA, if they were still there. Christman thought the trail looked different in the bright sunshine than it had the previous evening. But after reaching what he thought was a correct fork, Christman stood aside to rejoin 3rd Platoon as it came up.

Lieutenant Fox moved with the rest of the command group. They moved slowly, carefully, coming out of their night position, and angling down the jungle hillside into the valley below. The radios crackled now, and there were the sounds of canteens and rifles clattering.

After several hours, and after destroying a single enemy bunker, they reached the valley floor. As soon as Lieutenant Christman and his 3rd Platoon arrived at the creek bed, Christman approached Lieutenant Fox with news; Christman now realized that he'd had Alpha Company take a wrong fork in the trail. Christman had spotted the correct fork just prior to reaching the creek bed. However, the bunker had been the extent of enemy activity. It appeared to both Fox and Christman that since Alpha Company had not drawn fire except from the one enemy team, the NVA must have otherwise pulled out of the area. It appeared safe enough for the moment, and Alpha Company breathed a sigh of relief.

Above them, silent in the jungle mist, stood a young major of the North Vietnamese Army. He wore the pale green uniform and pith helmet of the northern forces, with red markings along the collar to show his rank. He looked to his left at one of his machine gun emplacements, and to his right at another. He could hear the Americans better than he could see them. They had come along the stream and into the narrow corridor that bunched them together along its bed.

The Americans would not be able to escape from that creek

bed, and the major knew that they would not even try. After almost four years of fighting the Americans, he had come to know their ways and to use that knowledge against them. The Americans would turn into the fire. They would come up the hillside into his positions in the mist, and he would get them all.

The heat was deepening, and each marine had sweated through the sateen fabric of his uniform. The valley floor was quiet along the streambed. Alpha Company filled their canteens, and some of the marines began opening C rations and drinking the cool stream water. As there was no further enemy contact, Lieutenant Fox radioed for a water detail to be sent down.

Everyone was low on water on the ridge, and the water detail's mission was to get water from the creek and carry it up to the ridgeline in canteens they had collected from individual marines. Fifteen marines from Charlie Company arrived a half-hour later and began filling canteens.

Lee Roy sat down on the brown cardboard of a C ration box, and opened the small green cans of crackers, pork, and pound cake. He looked up into the darkness of the jungle above them, and across the stream. He did not like it.

Looking down at Lee Roy, the North Vietnamese major drew his pistol out from its holster, ready to fire it, the signal for the ambush to start. But the marines had stopped. Their talking had become louder. The major could not believe his good fortune. The Marines were having lunch. He replaced the pistol in its holster, turned away from the view, and bent his head downward to speak into a radio handset carried by an enlisted man nearby. To the 82mm mortar crews on the next ridgeline to the west, he gave the coordinates of the streambed.

In the distance, a mortar tube could be heard to begin fire. The 82mm rounds began to explode in the treetops of the jungle canopy about Alpha Company. Due to the dense jungle and layers of limbs, the bursts were largely ineffective.

The water detail sergeant was hit by shrapnel in the face, and became hysterical. He screamed that he could not see, and he yelled for Lieutenant Fox to escort him and his detail back up the trail to the battalion area. Lieutenant Fox assigned Corporal Parnell of Second Squad, 2nd Platoon, to escort the water detail to the rear.

More 82mm rounds landed at both ends of the marines' position, flash-banging dust and vegetation into the air. Lee Roy stood transfixed, looking at the explosions and trying to comprehend what they meant. Friendly fire? All Lee Roy could think was, why would their own mortars be shelling them there along the A Shau?

Machine guns began to fire, sweeping down on them, raking along the creek bed, and marines began to fall. Screams began, screams that would not end. Men took cover behind trees, and began to fire their M16s up into the darkened hillside above.

Lieutenant Fox ordered 1st and 3rd Platoons to attack abreast, into the machine-gun fire. They attacked into the banana trees and thick brush of the hillside, and rifle fire on both sides became deafening.

The marine counterattack stalled in a crescendo of rifle and machine-gun fire. Lieutenant Fox moved forward to get a better feel for the tactical situation. He did not like the option of breaking contact while recovering wounded and dead marines under enemy gunfire. The other option, an all-or-nothing center attack by his reserve platoon, seemed the best under the circumstances. Lieutenant Fox yelled for the 2nd Platoon commander, Lieutenant Davis.

The noise level was tumultuous. There was firing, screaming, and the cracking fusillades of Vietnamese machine-gun fire churning the earth and tearing pieces out of anyone who stood erect. In the clearing where the company command group was situated, Lieutenant Fox quickly gave the order.

"First and Third Platoons are pinned down!" Fox screamed. "We've got to break through!" Fox shouted out the situational facts in short phrases. He bent down and drew positions in the dirt. First Platoon was on the left of the hillside. Third Platoon was on the right.

"They're throwing RPGs, grenades, sniper fire, everything from up here." Fox made a series of Xs in the earth along the facing area above his platoons. "There are machine guns here, and here, and here." Fox marked the positions in the ground using his finger.

Malone and Christman were with their platoons on the hillside, but Davis was there, a short distance from his 2nd Platoon that till then had been held in reserve. Lee Roy stood and listened intently to Lieutenant Fox.

"I want 2nd Platoon to attack here!" Fox drew a short line of advance from the creek bed up into the hillside, running into a draw or low ground between the positions of 1st and 3rd Platoons.

Fox was squatting, his finger pointing in the dirt, when the mortar round landed. It hit right next to the company command group, blasting everyone down and slashing at the earth and trees around them. Miraculously, Lee Roy stood unscathed near Lieutenant Fox. Around him, all were down: the company radio operator, the forward air controller, the battalion radio operator, the forward artillery observer, and Lieutenant Davis. Davis lay stunned and bleeding on the ground, with a gaping back wound. Doc Hudson knelt next to him, working to stanch the bleeding.

Pfc. Gary Winter, one of the battalion snipers assigned to Al-

pha Company, moved forward to pick up one of the radios, and
was knocked to the ground by a machine gun bullet.

Fox smacked Lee Roy on the shoulder. His eyes were wide and
there were red slashes of blood across his arms and shoulders.

"Did you hear the order, Herron?" he yelled, bringing his face
close to Lee Roy's.

"Yes, sir!" shouted Lee Roy.

"Well, you've got 2nd Platoon. Get going!" Fox yelled again,
and Lee Roy came to life, moving out across the streambed to the
jungle where 2nd Platoon was fighting for its life.

Across the clearing, bodies of marines lay everywhere. Second Platoon was little more than groups of men huddled together
against trees or lying flat on the ground. Some of the men were
moving and writhing, and some were still. Second Platoon was
down to seventeen effective men as Lee Roy worked his way
into its center, and crawled from position to position. He tied a
battle dressing tight across the leg wound of Pfc. Terry Presgrove,
who would remember this for the rest of his life.

Lee Roy urged them forward, but the machine gun bullets split
the air around them, pulverizing branches overhead. The men of
2nd Platoon could not go. They lay against the muddy ground
while enemy machine gun bullets passed above them. Lee Roy
lay flat with three of them, looking up into the mist and darkness above. There was death six inches above the wet berm they
lay against. Lee Roy listened to the whip-like cracking of bullets
above him.

Then he saw a hand in the bushes not more than ten feet from
them, a hand as if reaching down to get the marines. Lee Roy
looked at it, transfixed, and then the three enlisted men next to
him blasted the hand—and the arm attached to it and the foliage

around it—blasted it with their rifles, firing across Lee Roy's face, and his left ear went numb.

In the hand, Lee Roy saw something new and terrible. The enemy was coming for them. At least that one had come down the hillside for them, and there would have to be others. The North Vietnamese were coming down the hillside. Lee Roy looked about their position, and time slowed, and the clamor receded for a moment, and Lee Roy saw what suddenly seemed a very small number of desperate marines—no longer fighting but lying in the earth, trying to survive. If the North Vietnamese came down the hillside, if they got up out of their bunkers and came now, they would split the company in two between 1st and 3rd Platoons, and sweep the command group there across the clearing. The hand in the bush had been only ten feet away. They were coming.

Lee Roy turned back to the inferno on the hillside above. Now things were clearer to him—what had to be done and who had to do it. He lifted his head and peered up the hillside from under the edge of his camouflage helmet. He studied the patterns of the machine gun blasts. It was misty above them, but the machine gun fire was coming from certain positions. It wasn't coming from everywhere. Lee Roy took his glasses off, and in the heat and the confusion he rubbed them clear with his utility jacket sleeve. Then he put the glasses back on again and looked up again into the machine gun fire to pick out the lanes of the firing, which would lead him to the bunkers above.

The furthest marines forward in 2nd Platoon's position were on the left, maybe twenty or thirty yards from where Lee Roy lay. There were two of them there, partway up the hillside. Lee Roy rolled, got to his feet, and made for these two.

"Now, whatever happens, you stay with me today, Frankie," said Lenny Cosner. Stoppiello looked sideways at him, and Cosner yelled again, "'Cuz I'm really short and I'm not going to die today. And if you stay with me, you won't either!"

In the din of the gunfire, Cosner had to shout for Stoppiello to hear him.

They had advanced up the hillside into the ambush fire, and they had been shooting back into the lanes of the machine guns above. Now they were pinned down behind a rise in the ground.

Lee Roy rolled himself suddenly into their position.

"There's a machine gun bunker right up there!" screamed Lee Roy. "Who will come with me?" he shouted. The men looked back at him. Then Lance Cpl. Frank Stoppiello got to his knees. Cosner put his hand on Stoppiello's arm, but then he let it drop.

"I'll go with you, Lieutenant," said Stoppiello.

Through the haze and over the din of the firing, Lee Roy looked at Stoppiello and in his face he saw the face from the dream on Division Ridge, before he had come here. He reached out for Stoppiello, touched his shoulder. And then they were up and over the small mound of earth that had protected them.

In the mist and the dark of the canopied jungle, they moved down and behind the elements of 2nd Platoon, hunched over, Lieutenant Herron in the lead, slipping and sliding to the right, and then up the hillside. The firing of the enemy guns angled to their left some as they moved, and then they could see the bunker emplacement, maybe thirty yards away from them. They had positioned themselves on the flank of the bunker, and they had not been seen.

Lee Roy and Stoppiello went to their knees. Lee Roy pulled two grenades from the side of his pack and handed one to Stoppiello. "Aim for the window," he said near Stoppiello's ear. They pulled the pins. Lee Roy stood, and he heaved the steel bomb low and straight into the embrasure in front of the bunker, as long ago he had thrown a football straight and true in front of Coach Carson and his junior high teammates. Stoppiello threw too, and the explosions flash-banged, and the machine gun went silent.

Lee Roy moved out, up and across the ground behind the bunker, into the open space beyond, where another emplacement was churning and blasting down the ridgeline. Stoppiello followed just behind Lee Roy, watching apprehensively as the mist began to lift and the sun to reach the jungle floor.

Now, with the lifting mist, Lee Roy and Stoppiello stood out like two characters onstage. Lee Roy swung down his M16 and began to fire at this next bunker. Stoppiello fired too. And then, above the swath of sunlight in which they stood, the machine gun rotated toward them and blasted them both down the hillside.

Frank Stoppiello felt as if someone had smacked him in the back with a baseball bat, but then he felt no more pain. He tried to move his legs, but he could not feel them, and they did not move. He lay on his back on the wet hillside and looked for Lee Roy. Lee Roy lay just to his right, still and shattered, a gaping wound in his chest, a bullet hole in his forehead. His eyes were open, and he was looking at Stoppiello.

Around him, Stoppiello could see that other marines were coming now. Second Platoon was coming up the hill. Sgt. Dave Beyerlein, the platoon guide, was in the lead. He fired a Light Anti-tank Weapon (LAW) into another NVA machine gun bunker, and it erupted in smoke, flame, and flying fragments of brush. Beyerlein next turned and shot an NVA sniper out of a tree with another LAW rocket. The volume of hostile fire was diminishing.

A wounded but determined Lieutenant Fox contacted two OV-10 Bronco aircraft, and they came in, propeller airplanes, slow and accurate, blasting the hillside from just above the tree line and destroying the remaining machine gun bunker, the one that had felled Lee Roy Herron and Frank Stoppiello.

Alpha Company surged forward, up and through the enemy positions, shooting the living and kicking the dead.

Afterward there were more than one hundred NVA bodies that the marines had dragged into clearings to search.

It was over now. Those marines still alive felt numb and deaf, and suddenly awkward standing there looking at the carnage.

Bill Lawlis and another marine carried Lee Roy's body up the hillside to an open area the size of a baseball field, where the evacuation helicopters could get in. It was quiet there, and the sunlight now reached through the mists around them, and the light lay across Lee Roy where they set him down. They laid him next to the fallen Bill Christman, and they covered him with a poncho that had belonged to someone else. In Lee Roy's pocket was another letter, this one to his wife:

This little note is just my way of saying GoodBye. I'm so sorry, Danny, for causing you so much grief. God knows I never wanted to make you sad or unhappy. I believe it was God's Will that I serve as a Marine . . . that I die young . . . while defending our beloved America. . . . The one thing I ask of you is that you find some good Christian man and remarry. This is what I want with all my heart. We shared the greatest gift that God gives to His children on earth . . . stay true to the Lord and one day we shall meet in heaven.

Your Faithful Husband
Lee Roy

February 21, 1969

Dallas, Texas

Flat roofs are killers. I had always said that to my two law school friends, my roofer friends, and I said that several times each night during that week in February of 1969. "Killers." You can never really be sure where the leaks are in a flat roof. The part that looks terrible to you, standing up there on an apartment roof, looking down over the eaves to the lawns and sidewalks below—that may not be the bad part at all. You can just never tell.

We had a flat-roof job that week. The weather was cold, sometimes even freezing, in Dallas, but with mists like those Lee Roy faced eleven time zones around the world. I didn't know that at the time, but I have thought about it since.

We worked at roofing each day after law school, and we had to move things along because of the weather. You couldn't leave a job half done in those misty and drizzly conditions because it might otherwise leak.

We were working on one of those old, flat-roof apartment buildings that were built in the 1920s on the near north side of Dallas, during the expansion that came after World War I. It was three stories high. We had to push it that week, and I know we were all tired because we were going to law school during the day and studying at night after we had finished roofing for the day. We had done the scraping, laid mesh, and smoothed the tar out as quickly as we could. Mostly we didn't even break for dinner that week. Skies were gray, and we would look up at the clouds—it wasn't a good week.

One of the wives of the other law students brought dinner over. I remember these well, because they were the same each night: fried chicken and cans of Coca-Cola. I felt sorry for myself a couple of times that week, eating the fried chicken and sitting amidst tar cans. I felt sorry for myself because I hadn't thought about what Lee Roy might be going through.

I didn't know about Lee Roy.

One day, I remember, either February 21 or February 22, I was close to the edge of the roof, and not paying attention. There was a mist, and faint sheets of it blew across the tar I was scraping, laying a film of water across the oily surface. That can be really slippery. I stood up to change positions and slipped across the wet edge of the roof, and suddenly I was falling. I remember yelling out and recall the feeling of the inevitability of the fall, and I remember that I closed my eyes and let things go. I was falling and there was no stopping it.

Many years later I wondered if I had fallen at about the same time that Lee Roy had been killed. It was hard to know, because of the International Date Line and all. There is no accounting for strange ideas like that, so I have always tried to put them out of my mind, but this one did stay with me, creeping back now and then into my consciousness. Maybe Lee Roy and I had fallen at about the same time, on opposite sides of the earth.

As I've gotten older, I am sometimes up in the middle of the night and sometimes wonder about it: whether Lee Roy was already dead when I fell, or if his death came just after, or whether we fell at the same time in different places, one living and one dying. As useless as it may be to think of things this way, Lee Roy and I both fell that month and that year, and one of us lived and one of us died. That's how it has seemed to me.

The next thing I remember after I went over the edge was the sound of sirens, then riding in the back of an ambulance and kind of waking up in the emergency room at Parkland Hospital. I remember a doctor placing a towel over my head and sewing up my chin, and explaining to me that I had landed on my left side and that the rain and mist had softened the ground and so I had lived, when by rights I should have died. I had been working in one of my Marine Corps PLC utility shirts, and the doctor said there would be blood on the uniform now. And then the doctor was done and he walked out of the cubicle, leaving me with the nurse to take the towel off my face. I remember standing up from the gurney, and there was a mirror in the old Parkland emergency room, where they had brought Jack Kennedy to die six years before, and I looked at myself in the Marine Corps shirt and saw the blood across the front of it. I threw the shirt away after I got home.

Someone called Martie, and she came down and found me wandering in the halls of the emergency room, dazed and trying to figure out how to check out.

My head hurt, my chin hurt, and my chest hurt. I had some broken ribs, and my head didn't work straight, and for many months afterward I just did not feel right. Life went on and I had to return to law school, but I stopped the roofing work and figured we would just have to borrow more.

Later I came to wonder if Lee Roy had felt anything that day. If it had hurt or if he had seen his foot go up in the air as he fell like I had seen mine.

Most of all, as the years have passed, I have wondered if Lee Roy felt alone during those last minutes, knowing how far he was from home. That part has bothered me the most.

[13]
1970–1997
Life without Lee Roy

It takes time to tell the story of a man who dies young, but only a few pages to tell about an old man. That would be my story, the story about me without Lee Roy.

I'll start with the children. "Children are your only true legacy," my paternal grandfather, the one who was the cotton farmer, used to say. If you live a long time, for most of us that turns out to be true.

Amy LaVerne Nelson came to us on the night of August 27, 1971. The doctors make notes about these things: "2 Kg Caucasian female, NSVD [normal spontaneous vaginal delivery], APGAR 10 [top score for beating heart, working lungs, and pink color]." But the medical notes and the numbers didn't capture the real story of Amy Nelson, a new person who came into the world as our daughter.

I remember that night. The winds blew and the rains pelted down from Tropical Storm Doria. Martie and I were in Newport, Rhode Island, where I had been assigned to the Naval Justice School after graduating from law school. The hospital was full at the Newport naval station that night, and Martie was in labor, so we had to drive down the coast to a small hospital in Westerly.

I dropped Martie off at the emergency room entrance to the hospital, and I parked the car. I had to walk in the rain across the parking lot, bending my head down, feeling the rain lash my shoulders and legs—then looking up to see the lights of the hospital doors gleaming. I had forgotten my raincoat when I walked inside, and I must have looked like a character from *The Moonstone* (the book some say was the first detective novel).

Looking back at the past there now seems inevitability about my having finished law school. Sometimes I tell people that I went to law school, and it seems to fit neatly into those few words. "I went to the law school at Southern Methodist University and graduated in 1970." But time makes things sound easier than they were.

The doors of Westerly Hospital slid open, and one of the nurses took me right upstairs to the second floor, where the delivery rooms were. Martie was already there, sitting up in a bed, with all kinds of trays and instruments about. A gray-haired nurse with an Irish accent was already fussing with stirrups and stools at the foot of the bed. It was coming quick. Even I could see that.

"Come on in then, laddie," said the nurse. She didn't look at me, still busy fitting stainless steel elbows into slots at the base of the bed.

"Oh," I said, and I remember starting to back up, small steps backward at the threshold of the room.

"Well, aren't ya goin' to be present at the arrival of your baby?" she asked, still looking more at Martie than at me.

Martie looked apprehensive. She was gripping the rails of the bed and breathing deeply.

"Of carse you are!" said the nurse, answering her own question. "Here," she said, and she took me by the hand, while pushing a white linen mask up against my face. "You sit here and hold onto your wife's hand," and she led me to a red plastic chair by the head of the bed.

I sat down. I held Martie's hand. The obstetrician came in. I never did know his name. The nurse went around to the other side of the bed and held Martie's other hand for a time. She coached Martie on her breathing. The baby—Amy—came. The obstetrician held her up. The nurse placed a small white stocking cap on her head. And Amy looked at me, I'm sure she looked at me with those small dark baby eyes. Amy LaVerne Nelson sat there naked and pink in the obstetrician's hands, a stocking cap on her head, and she looked at me.

To me, Amy was beautiful from that first moment, when she looked at me. And, in a way, she has never changed: she has always seemed just right.

I had finished the SMU School of Law in the spring of 1970, and Martie and I had moved to Houston for a few months, for a temporary job that I had with Ernst and Ernst, the accounting firm, before I had to report to The Basic School. That temporary job included helping with an interim audit of Houston Endowment that started a relationship between me and the endowment, one that has continued to the present.

The Uniform Code of Military Justice had been amended in 1968, so that military lawyers could not report for active duty until they had passed the bar exam, so Martie and I thought we would see a new place, and spend some time in Houston, until my results from the Texas bar came. To us it was a great adventure, moving to Houston, with its great buildings and parks, and the Gulf nearby so that some days when the wind was right you could smell the salt. When you're young and just married, even little things are new and interesting.

My bar results arrived in September. I had passed. I had already signed up for the certified public accountant examination that November, so the Marine Corps extended us in Houston until January of 1971. I was getting paid. The war in Vietnam was winding down, and I didn't think I would have to go. Life seemed good. We started to think about having a family, Martie and I.

I had no thoughts of Lee Roy during that time. None.

Getting back to that August night in Rhode Island, the obstetrician set Amy on Martie's chest. Martie was given some kind of shot. The nurse wrapped Amy in a little cotton blanket. Someone started to take the steel stirrups down from the bed. Amy was taken away to the nursery. Martie looked totally exhausted. I was ushered out of the delivery room and told to come back after a while. The nurse peeked her head around the delivery room door as I left.

"Ya done good!" she said. It wasn't clear to me that I had done anything.

I walked out into the hospital hallway. There's about nothing as long and quiet as a hospital hallway at night. It's a totally different thing from a hospital hallway in the day. And I remember the strange smell, a smell that made me think no germs could ever live there because the air itself would kill them off. I was trying to understand what was happening to me, with Amy's birth and all. It was Amy who had been born, but I had changed. It was too confusing to make sense of. I decided to walk.

The hospital was laid out in a large H, and I walked the crosspiece of the H, away from the birthing rooms and the nursery, to the gynecology floor on the other side. Here there were rows of rooms, and lights were on in some of them. There were two nurses in the hall, and a medication cart. Something was happening inside the room in front of them. The same doctor, the one I had considered the obstetrician, emerged from the lit room and spoke quietly to the nurses. They nodded. The doctor looked up and saw me standing there looking. He stared at me, and in his look was a great sadness. I had to look away. I had made a mistake to come here. In the rush and the joy of Amy's birth I had felt that the entire hospital must be joyful, but it was not so. Over here, across the connecting hall from the delivery rooms, things were different. Some of the doctors and the nurses were the same people, but it felt different over here. I didn't belong. I saw it in the way that doctor looked at me. I had been wrong to cross over.

I turned around and went back to the obstetric part of the floor, and down the stairs to the small lobby of the hospital. I sat down there, on a leather chair surrounded by parquet floor, alone in the early morning hours of August 28, and I watched the rain pelting the windows. I did think of Lee Roy that night, after the delivery was over, and after I had moved down to the lobby and was alone. I tell people that I didn't think of Lee Roy during those years, but that isn't true. Pieces of Lee Roy would come back to me at certain times, like sitting there in the Westerly Hospital lobby, with the rains of Tropical Storm Doria pelting the parking lot outside, and our first child just born. Shadows of Lee Roy came back to me that night, but he wasn't in his uniform. This is embarrassing to write, but as I looked out into the waves of rain, I thought I could see Lee Roy standing just beyond the lights from the lobby. I couldn't see him clearly, because the rain was so strong, and it was so dark. But I thought I could see him, as if he were out there in the rain watching me, curious about what was happening. He was looking at me, I know he was looking at me that night when Amy was born. Yes, he was there. He seemed elevated and larger than I had remembered him, kind

of shimmering in the little lights from the rain. And to my relief, he seemed—how can I put this without your thinking I've
gone over the top?—he seemed approving of me, maybe even
proud of me or glad for me for how things had gone after we
had parted. That meant a lot to me, because I hadn't really been
sure how he would have felt about it all, my being alive, having a
career, having a family—and my not going to Vietnam. That was
the worst thing that sometimes came to me: the thought that by
not going I had let Lee Roy down.

After a time, I got up from the chair, went to the vending machine at the corner of the lobby, and put two quarters in, and the
machine made a small cup of thin coffee. After the sun came up,
I went back up to the second floor.

Martie was situated in a new room. She was sitting up, and
she was smiling. She had combed her hair, and she had put on
her makeup. She looked beautiful.

The nurse was still there, standing by Martie's bed.

"Well, good marnin' to ya, Mr. Nelson," she said.

It didn't feel that good to me, after sitting and dozing in the
lobby till dawn.

"Are the two of you ready to see yar daughter this marnin'?"
she asked.

Martie smiled.

"Well I'll get her, then. And it'll be time for her breakfast, I
might add," said the nurse, and she was out the door.

Martie reached her hand up to me. I sat down in the chair next
to her. We held hands, and we waited to meet our daughter.

The nurse brought Amy. She was wrapped in a small yellow
blanket. Her face was reddish. The nurse helped Martie with
the breastfeeding. I sat by Martie, in the dim light of the new
day, and I watched our daughter nurse. The rain outside was

Lieutenant David Nelson is pictured here as a student at The Basic School (TBS) in March 1971. All Marine Corps officers, including attorneys, must attend TBS as their first duty station. Official U.S. Marine Corps photo.

stopping. The storm was passing. Amy was there. Martie was there. I felt a surge of happiness pass through me, looking at them.

My Basic School class had just finished the month before, and I had then reported to the naval base in Newport for Naval Justice School. The shadows of the Marine Corps ordeal in Vietnam hung over everything we did in The Basic School in 1971. Our instructors had been selected for their experiences in Vietnam, and most of them wore the big medals of personal heroism. Oliver North and Wesley Fox were among my instructors, but I didn't know then that Captain Fox had commanded in the action where Lee Roy had died. I tried not to think about Lee Roy as we went through the six months of TBS—tried not to wonder if he might have held this rifle that I held or sat in this chair that I sat in. I did not want to know where Lee Roy's room had been in O'Bannon Hall. I was assigned MOS 4402—Judge Advocate General Corps. It came automatically, because I was a lawyer—I didn't have to attend MOS Day that year.

I did okay in TBS, finishing in the middle of the class. Martie and I lived in an apartment off base, since I was older than the others and was married. Almost all of the others attending were second lieutenants, but I was already a captain. I even outranked some of the instructors, who had returned from the Vietnam War but had not yet been promoted from first lieutenant to captain. At times it was awkward, but I kept some distance from it all.

When Amy nursed that first time in the hospital, her eyes closed, I watched her small red hands lifted in the air. When she was done, Martie rewrapped her in the yellow blanket and set her in the angle of her arm, and Amy sat up a little, and there were three of us. After a time, the nurse came to take Amy back to the nursery, and I started to cry. I couldn't remember when I'd last cried. The nurse wheeled little Amy out of the room, and I tried to hide my tears.

"Wive goodbye to har!" said the nurse as she pushed Amy out the door in the clear plastic bassinet. And Martie and I waved as Amy left us.

Martie took my hand again. "You know," she said, "Amy will always be leaving us, a little more each year, if we do our job as parents right." I was trying to hide my tears from Martie, so she wouldn't see. But she had seen, and she had understood, as the nurse took Amy from us.

"She doesn't belong to us, David," said Martie. "God has only . loaned her to us for a short time. Our job is to get her ready so that she can become the person she wants to be."

I nodded, but it was still hard to see a little, because of the tears.

Sometimes now when I see Amy, who is grown up and a lawyer like me, I can still faintly hear the sound the wind made that night in August when she came to us. She is now married to Patrick J. Concannon, a U.S. Navy Submarine Force veteran, and they have a son, Zackery.

When Naval Justice School was over in October 1971, I received orders to the 2nd Marine Division at Camp Lejeune, North Carolina. It was a strange time for the Marine Corps, and I had almost no sooner arrived at Camp Lejeune, it seemed, than I received new orders to report to the 3rd Marine Division on Okinawa. That was in late 1972.

Okinawa: For me it was a twelve-month stay on a rocky island, in a small apartment with a pagoda roof. There were military courts for fighting and drunkenness, and one or two for desertion. There were some discharges. I wore the short-sleeve khaki uniform with the USMC field jacket over it on cold days. Martie and Amy came for half the year, even though dependents were officially forbidden to stay for more than two months, according to 3rd Marine Division policy.

I wondered at the time if Lee Roy had seen that I was violating policy by having Martie and Amy stay. I felt just a little ashamed, thinking that he might have. This was Lee Roy's division, the 3rd. The 9th Marine Regiment was bivouacked just up the road at Camp Schwab, but I never went there.

Outside the big Kadena Air Base, on the southern part of the island, there was a long trench-like area filled with Vietnam War wreckage: trucks, jeeps, parts of aircraft, piles of boxes, and unrecognizable hunks of metal. The equipment had been "down south," as they called Vietnam on Okinawa, and now lay there as if forbidden to return to the United States because of what it had done or been through. Most people probably didn't notice or think much of this mechanical cemetery, partly because it was somewhat sunken and only the top showed. I noticed but didn't like to look at it. Something about it made me sad, as if the machines were weeping about what had happened and the way they had been left behind. When Martie, Amy, and I drove south on the island, I always took a different road so I didn't have to see it.

Then it came time for us to go home. That's the way I thought of it. We didn't actually have a home at that time, though. We had Amy, and we had each other, but we didn't have much else. I think when we talked about going home, we were then picturing Houston, where we had spent those months in 1970, where Martie and I had started our lives together. Ernst and Ernst, the big accounting firm (now Ernst and Young), had said that I could join them when I came back, and that's what Martie and I decided we would do. We would go back to Houston, and I would work for Ernst and Ernst in their tax department. We would buy a house, and we would raise our family there. We would do all those things that Lee Roy and Danny had never gotten to do. When I walked up the aluminum steps to the Continental airplane at Kadena, to go home, I turned a little and looked back to see if Lee Roy were watching me. That part of leaving Asia didn't feel good that day.

Just before I entered the plane, I looked back again and said goodbye—to Lee Roy. I was kind of hunched over, and turned away from the others there, so I don't think they heard. I didn't talk like that with Lee Roy very often. After that I didn't think of Lee Roy for a very long time.

So Martie and I came home to the United States, I got out of the Marine Corps, we moved to Houston, and I went to work for Ernst and Ernst as a certified public accountant and attorney. I worked in the area of estates, trusts, and tax-exempt organizations, because I had the unusual credentials of both law and accounting.

I can remember my military times, our wedding, and Amy's birth, like photos you see that make you suddenly feel you could cross right over and become who you were before, but I can't remember my post–Marine Corps years well. Two decades of the seventies and eighties just seem to have passed. We had a house in Houston: white bricks, three bedrooms, two bathrooms, a big fireplace for the few cold days in the year. I worked. Martie took care of the house and the family. Amy grew up and went to school. Our second child, Rachel, came to us on June 30, 1985—I remember that clearly. But I don't remember much of the detail of those years.

Mostly I worked hard. By 1978, Ernst and Ernst had become Ernst and Whinney. I was determined to make partner there, and so I worked.

I remember one summer, probably around 1980, when I took a long weekend and we vacationed at a Texas lake. We were picnicking by the lake, and Amy was splashing in it, but I left the family and walked up the hill to the car, to study some briefing papers concerning an estate. I think Martie took that a bit hard, me sitting there in the car studying papers, while she played with Amy on vacation. And I did feel a little bad about that, but I became a full partner at the firm in 1981, after only eight years. That was something. What I said to myself about that was that there had to be some tradeoff in the family; to have a husband and father who was a full partner at Ernst and Whinney, the family had to give up some things, too. That's what I said to myself at the time.

But after a while I learned that success at work was a mixed thing.

In 1989 Ernst and Whinney merged with Arthur Young to become Ernst and Young, and soon after that I was fired. There had been an error in the estate documents of an elderly client we were managing, and I guess it was my fault. I just didn't see it. The legal guardian of the client sued the firm over it, and even though to me it didn't seem like such a big problem, Ernst and Young wasn't going to tolerate the adverse publicity. I remember joking about it to my managing partner at the time, saying that there wasn't any such thing as bad publicity, but I could tell he didn't think it was funny (and that he didn't agree).

What I remember most is that I refused to resign, as the firm asked me to do, and the managing partners were shocked by this. It took them a couple of months to figure out what to do, and then finally they got their courage up and fired me, and they concocted one of those baloney internal memos about how I "had decided to take advantage of another exciting opportunity elsewhere," or something like that.

I don't know why I refused to resign. The firing hurt. It is one thing to hear that everybody in business probably has to be fired once in a career, but it is difficult. When it happens, if you're the kind of person I've tried to be, you have to bounce back, make the best of it, because you know your family depends on you.

And that's what I did. They remembered me at Houston Endowment, and I became vice president and grant director there. Here was good fortune. Houston Endowment is the largest private philanthropic organization in Texas. It was founded by Jesse Holman Jones and Mary Gibbs Jones in 1937 to make gifts to schools, colleges, and charitable organizations. I had the greatest job in the world, managing the process of giving grants to support many good works in Texas. I never met Jesse or Mary Gibbs, but I always felt proud to be associated with them through the endowment. One story about Jesse I remember. He had been appointed secretary of commerce by Franklin Roosevelt, in FDR's third term, and after Pearl Harbor the Joneses were some of the first people whom FDR and Eleanor had to the White House for an informal dinner. There FDR had shared his anxiety about having enough oil for the great war that had begun, and Jesse Jones leaned across the dinner table and said, "Texas will take care of all the oil that you need, Mr. President." I felt very proud about that story, working for the endowment. (As I write this, I have returned to Houston Endowment, doing some part-time consulting work.)

After I was fired I had to rethink the way I felt about work. I had given so much to it, but then I saw how it could turn on you, disappoint. And Rachel was there now. I was starting to change.

One strange thing happened when I was about fifty. Maybe it was 1996. I was sitting in my office at Houston Endowment, looking out the windows across the treetops and streets of the city, just daydreaming, when suddenly I sat up in the leather swivel chair because I thought I had heard someone say my name. This may seem far out, but I think it was Lee Roy—and thought that at the time. I consciously thought about Lee Roy then, which I hadn't really done since his death.

Nothing more came. I sat still there in the chair and waited for something more, but there was nothing more. I never said anything about this, and probably things like this happen to everyone. But I thought about it without knowing what it had meant.

Maybe it was my being fifty, or something related to that: from that day I thought of Lee Roy more, but in a strange way because I envied Lee Roy a little. What Lee Roy had done had been difficult for a day, I thought, but what I had needed to do with my work and family and politics had been difficult for twenty-five years, and there was no prospect of it ending. And there was self-doubt from time to time. Lee Roy had never had to face that, I thought. And so I envied him for a short time at around age fifty, but this passed.

The self-doubt, the rethinking of work, led me to feel suddenly that I had to spend more time with my daughter Rachel. By that time Amy was in college at Texas A&M, but Rachel was still at home.

Rachel was different from Amy, even from the beginning. She always liked taking care of things, like small animals and sad people. She brought home a runaway cat, one time, when she was in high school. It was probably from the game of counting cats I had taught her, while we were out jogging on the streets and sidewalks of the city. We called this one a runaway cat, but it was really a feral cat. We took that wild cat into our house, and he didn't last that long in the civilized world, getting run over by a car before long. Rachel was shattered by it. We didn't let her see the cat's body, just told her about it after she got home from school one day. She cried for hours about that cat she had named Huxley. That's just the way Rachel was—and is. (As I write this she is preparing to work in the medical field.)

I wanted to make sure I did more things with Rachel, because I was at a different stage in life than when Amy had been young. Rachel and I jogged in the neighborhood each morning before school. At first, I had to play games with Rachel to keep her attention while we ran, like the cat-counting game mentioned above. (One morning we counted twelve cats in that neighborhood.) Then we would name the colors of houses. As months went by, Rachel went faster and faster, and she could outrun me after about a year. She liked running, developed with it, and by middle school joined the track team as its youngest member. In meets she ran the quarter mile and the half. In the summer, I would come home early from work three days a week and take her to a running camp at Stratford High School in Houston.

I liked the way things developed with Rachel and me. I drove her to school most days and we would sing along with songs on the radio. We listened to an "oldies" station and sang Motown songs. Rachel especially liked the Supremes, I remember.

I went to all of her track meets in middle school. Martie came many times, too. Sitting there in the bleachers watching Rachel, I felt good about things, as did Martie, although we didn't talk about it. When things are going well, I've always felt no need to say it.

I had no visitations from Lee Roy during those years. When I did think about him, I thought how much he had missed because of what had happened that day in 1969. And how hard much of it had been. Lee Roy had missed that particular hard part.

One difficult thing about being a parent is that there are no report cards. Children don't give you one, exactly, and you really can't ask them for one. Would it be right to come over to your daughter after dinner, sit down next to her, and ask her how you're doing as a parent? No. You have to watch, wait, and listen to see whether you've done it the right way, and sometimes what feels right at the time turns out not to be right later. I worried some about Amy, about the way I had been in my drive to make partner and all. I wondered about it.

Much later Amy told me a story out of the blue. We had been sitting in my study, just talking. By this time she was a lawyer, having gone to the law school at St. Mary's in San Antonio. "Do you remember that time, Dad," she said, "when I had to take the bar exam in Pasadena? I drove out there, and you drove behind me, in case I had car trouble, or a flat tire?"

I did remember. It hadn't seemed like anything to me at the time, but now I could see that it had been something.

"Then," continued Amy, "On the first day of the bar you stood there in the hallway with me and my nervous friends while we waited for the doors to open?"

I remembered.

"You drove all that way, just to stand there with me and my friends that morning," Amy continued. "And then you stood in line with me while they searched my bags and checked my ID."

Amy sat across from me, in one of the chairs in my study in our Houston house. She has blue eyes, and she looks a little like I do, I guess. I could see it that day, sitting there.

"You stood out there in the foyer and you watched me through the glass doors after I went in," she said.

I remembered that. It had seemed silly to me, standing there in the lobby with Amy and her friends, all of them nervous and chattering. I had tried desperately to think of what to say—the right thing to say. But I hadn't been able to think of anything. At difficult times, I'm not much of a talker.

"And you followed me the next two days of the bar exam, too," said Amy. "You made sure I made it safely to the exam each day."

It was true. I had followed her there each day.

"I always wanted to tell you 'thank you' for that day, Dad," she said. "And that day was like many others," she said. "You were always there for me."

Neither of us said too much after that. I felt a lot better, though. Children say things at funny times, the things you want to hear and the things you need to hear.

I felt better about Amy after that.

By about 1997 Martie and I figured that the hard times were over. Sitting at a small table in a French restaurant in Houston on New Year's Eve, 1996, toasting our lives and our family, I remember that we said that: "Our hard times are over."

I'll never say that again, on New Year's Eve or at any other time. Because even as we said it—as I said it—something seemed to move inside me. I just felt this twinge, that I had said something that wasn't right.

Colonel Fox was listening. Sitting there in that Borders bookstore café, with small cups of espresso in front of us, he had been listening. I'm not usually that much of a talker, but that day I had talked and Colonel Fox had listened. I had forgotten the espresso. I picked up the small cup. I looked down. I did not want to see Colonel Fox's face.

"Lee was my lieutenant," said Colonel Fox. "He will always be my lieutenant," he said.

I did not want to see Colonel Fox cry. That's why I wasn't looking up.

"You didn't let Lee down, David," said Colonel Fox.

I looked up at him, across the tiny cup. He wasn't crying. If anything, he had brightness in his eyes. He was talking to me. He had understood me.

"And you didn't let me down, David," said the colonel.

I just looked at Colonel Fox. I was trying to understand him. I looked into the deep wrinkles and the scars in his face, and I thought of all the pain, deprivation, and violence behind those wrinkles.

"But it won't mean anything for me to tell you that," he said.

I was staring at him. The rimless glasses, the blue eyes, the

Medal of Honor around his neck. I couldn't understand what he was saying.

"Lee will have to tell you that, David," said the colonel.

This man was a leader, I could feel it. It wasn't just that he had the big medal, which had come to him through some accident of time and place. It hadn't been an accident. This man was turning my life with his words, as he must have turned lives that day in 1969 when so many died, but so many lived.

"You will have to find Lee," he said. "Find him inside yourself, and ask him if it was okay, the way you did it."

There were undulating waves across my line of vision. I felt briefly that I was floating free from time and place.

"You'll have to ask Lee to let you go," said the colonel.

And then he pushed back his chair and stood up. I sat still and couldn't believe he was leaving. After all the talking I had done, this man had said just these words and no others. Now I don't know who I am, I thought. He can't just stand up and leave now. But he did. Colonel Fox pushed his chair under the table and walked off, placing his hand on my shoulder briefly as he went.

[14]
1997–2001
The Search for Lee Roy

Frank Stoppiello would know. That's what I told myself. I knew that Stoppiello had been with Lee Roy in those last minutes, because it was in Colonel Fox's book. Frank Stoppiello would know what had really happened that day in A Shau Valley in 1969, and when I knew what had really happened, then I would be okay. That's what I told myself. I would find Frank Stoppiello, and he would tell me what I needed to know.

But it turned out that it wasn't easy to find Frank Stoppiello. I had thought that I would call the Department of the Navy, and that someone there would give me Frank's number down in Mexico, and that I would call him, and then go down to visit him. Maybe we would sit together in a stucco café, and there would be cold lime-juice drinks in front of us, and we would talk it all out for hours. But that wasn't how it turned out.

Frank Stoppiello had completed his physical rehabilitation, then moved to Guadalajara, Mexico, Colonel Fox thought, and that was probably where he still lived. That's all I could find out in the beginning, and I never got much further with it.

I thought it would be easy to locate Stoppiello, because he would still be drawing his disability pension. But you can't just call or write the Department of the Navy and get someone's address. I tried it several times. There are all kinds of rules about privacy, which I guess make sense for other people, but in late 1997 I felt that they shouldn't apply to me, shouldn't prevent what I was trying to do. The best I could get from them was a promise to forward a note from me to Stoppiello, and he could decide if he wanted to connect with me. That was what I wanted. I wanted to get close to someone who had been there with Lee Roy on his last day.

But Stoppiello didn't reply to any of my letters. I tried e-mails to be forwarded. I tried telephone messages to be relayed. He didn't reply.

Next, I got Lee Roy's Navy Cross citation from Colonel Fox:

For extraordinary heroism while serving as Executive Officer, Company A, First Battalion, Ninth Marines, Third Marine Division in the Republic of Viet Nam on 22 February 1969. While patrolling north of Ashau Valley in Quang Tri Province, the lead elements of Company A came under intense fire and were pinned down by a large North Vietnamese Army force. First Lieutenant Herron maneuvered one of his platoons forward to reinforce the lead elements. When the second platoon commander was seriously wounded, he immediately assumed command and quickly organized the men into an assault force. Skillfully deploying his men, he led them in an aggressive attack until halted and pinned down by an extremely heavy volume of cross-fire from several enemy machine guns augmented by mortar, rocket-propelled grenade, small arms, and automatic weapons fire from the North Vietnamese emplacements, as well as numerous sniper positions in trees in the dense jungle canopy. Undaunted by the hostile rounds impacting around him, First Lieutenant Herron repeatedly exposed himself to enemy fire as he moved among his men to encourage them and urged them to inch forward to positions from which they could deliver more effective return fire. Aware that the fire from two mutually supporting hostile machine guns was holding his Marines in place and preventing the removal of the casualties, he completely disregarded his own safety as he exposed himself to North Vietnamese fire to direct a light antitank assault round which scored a direct hit on one of the machine gun bunkers. Boldly leaping to his feet, he fearlessly charged across the fire-swept terrain to hurl hand grenades and fire his weapon against the enemy emplacement, killing nine North Vietnamese soldiers who were in the bunker. While directing his men in the assault on the remaining bunker, First Lieutenant Herron was mortally wounded by enemy sniper fire. His heroic actions inspired his men to such aggressive action in coordinated company attack that 105 North Vietnamese soldiers were killed and the large bunker complex destroyed. By his courage, bold initiative and unwavering devotion to duty, First Lieutenant Herron upheld the highest traditions of the Marine Corps and the United States Naval Service. He gallantly gave his life for his country.

I read the words of the citation again and again. I sat alone in my study at night after Martie had gone to bed, reread the words, and tried to understand what they meant. Death stops things, freezes them like a photograph does, and then you have to study each detail in the picture to understand it. Sometimes I would just sit and stare at the words, waiting for them to tell me more about that day so long ago, the day that Lee Roy died.

"What are you doing, David?"

Martie had walked up behind me. I hadn't heard her coming. I was sitting in my study at Christmastime in 1997.

"Oh," I said. I didn't know what to say. I was a little embarrassed. "I was just thinking," I said.

Martie sat down in an old leather chair off to the side, a chair in which the girls had often sat.

"You're thinking about Lee Roy, aren't you, David?" she said.

I looked out the window. It wasn't as if there was much to see out there. Our backyard. Some trees. The neighbors' houses. Had Lee Roy missed much?

"What are these boxes, David?" asked Martie. I looked back. There were cardboard boxes along one wall of the study. I had them labeled with little stick-on notes, one note and one box for different things about Lee Roy: "High School Friends," "Navy Department," and others.

"Oh," I said. "Those are for Lee Roy."

"You're going to have to find Lee Roy," Martie said. She always spoke softly, but I had heard what she said. I did not look at her. I was looking at the boxes.

"I just want you to know that I understand that," she said. "I think I always thought this time would come, and you would go looking for him. It will be all right." And she left the study and went back downstairs.

I stared out the window again. I wasn't 100 percent sure what I was looking for.

And then one day a letter came from Frank Stoppiello:

Dear Mr. Nelson,

I am sorry I haven't written sooner. I was out of town most of the summer and just checked my P.O. Box and found your letter.

I was with your friend Lt. Herron when he was killed.

I will start from when I was with Lenny Cosner because before that I hadn't seen Lt. Herron.

Lenny and I were on the left flank of 2d platoon when Lt. Herron told me to go with him, not as a radioman because we had no radio. We moved behind 2d platoon where Lt. Herron got the platoon on line to assault the bunker. Lt. Herron and I took up positions on the right flank of the platoon. As we started forward the enemy fire increased. Lt. Herron told me to follow him and we moved to the right and forward to flank the enemy position.

At the same time 2d platoon was also moving forward but at a slower pace as they were under heavier fire than Lt. Herron and I were at that time. We got into position and lobbed grenades at the bunker. As soon as we lobbed our grenades we were fired upon from another bunker. We both returned fire at the new position. That is when Lt. Herron was hit. He was killed instantly. I was hit a few seconds after.

You can tell his mother and sister that he did not suffer. He died without pain.

I am sorry that you lost your friend Mr. Nelson.

I am proud to have served with Lt. Herron. If I can be of further service to you just let me know. Your friend and brother Marine.

Sincerely,

Frank Stoppiello

Stoppiello also enclosed a map he'd drawn. This helped me. The hand that drew it had been there that day. I studied the diagram. Every night for a while in 1998 I laid it on my desk after dinner, and studied every mark carefully. I tried to feel what Lee Roy must have felt at each step, pulling back out of the line on the left side of 2nd Platoon, and moving along the angle of the slope to the right, hunched over, slipping and sliding, moving through

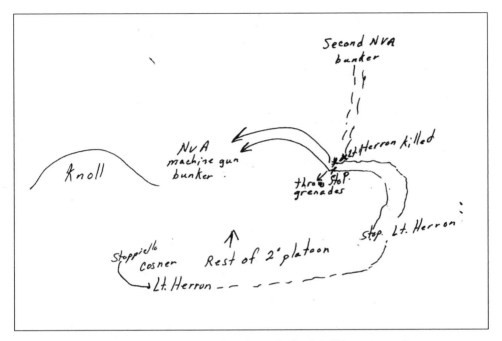

Frank Stoppiello drew this diagram that shows the battlefield in A Shau Valley, Vietnam, on February 22, 1969, where Lee Roy Herron was killed and Stoppiello severely wounded. Author's personal collection.

a sea of gunfire and pandemonium to the open area below the enemy machine guns. Did he know what was coming? Did he say anything? Stoppiello would know.

But there was something terribly missing from his letter: a return address. I knew immediately what it meant. There would be nothing more from Frank Stoppiello. I tried a few more inquiries through the Department of Veterans Affairs, but nothing more came of it. This was all I would ever hear from Stoppiello.

For weeks that winter I thought of going to Guadalajara to find him. I thought of how I would do it. I checked the airlines. There was a nonstop flight daily from Houston's George Bush Airport, via Aero Mexico, to Guadalajara, and there was a Holiday Inn in Guadalajara—two of them, actually. I would check into one, and ask the front desk people to help me. Surely, Frank Stoppiello must have a telephone, I thought. And once I found his number in a phone book, I would call him. The phone would ring, and then he would answer.

There I came up against a problem. In my mind's ear, I could hear everything right up to Stoppiello's answering the phone, but I couldn't think of what would happen next. I couldn't think of what I would say or what he might say. I brooded about this for a while.

"He doesn't want to talk with you, David."

Startled, I turned around in my chair. Martie was sitting behind me in the study.

"He's not going to tell you anything more about Lee Roy," she said. As ever, Martie was sure, calm, and right.

"And it's not because he doesn't want to help you, David," she continued. "It's because he can't," she said. "In a way," she went on, turning away from me a little, "he died too that day, David. At least the Frank Stoppiello you want to meet and speak with died that day."

I felt emptiness. Martie was right. But I felt a terrible sadness about it, and loneliness. The one person who had been with Lee Roy when he died, that person was gone, too.

"I know you've been thinking about going down there to Guadalajara, David," she said.

I nodded.

"And what if you did that?" asked Martie. "What if you got on the plane, and went down there and you hired some taxi driver and you spent the whole day looking for Frank Stoppiello, and you found him? What then?" asked Martie.

I was looking out the window, seeing some fleeing clouds.

"What would you ask him, David? What would you ask Frank Stoppiello, that you don't already know?"

The clouds were moving fast and low above the horizon, moving into Houston from the west.

"You know what happened that day, David."

I wondered if it was going to rain.

I looked back from the window. I looked at Martie now, and I faced what she was saying.

"Each person has to find his own way with these things, David," she said. "Frank Stoppiello has found his way, and he's not going back there again to that day in 1969."

I turned her words in my mind.

"He sent you that letter, and the map. That's as far as he can go with this."

Martie paused.

"Frank has found his way with this, David. He's become someone new out of that day almost thirty years ago. But it is private who he is now. He doesn't want anyone from that day to see him. And he doesn't want to see them."

Martie stopped. I didn't like what she had said. I felt a terrible emptiness inside.

Martie stood up, came over, and hugged me. Then it was dinnertime.

I thought maybe it would all go away for me after that day, the day Martie came up to my study to talk with me. Houston Endowment was busy with its grant cycles, and I tried to get back into it, to live in the here and now of 1998.

This worked somewhat, for a while. I did work for Houston Endowment at the Jones Building. Martie and I went to plays and PTA meetings at Rachel's middle school. On weekends, I cleaned the garage, over and over. Then in April I went to Washington to see John H. Dalton, secretary of the navy.

I was only seeing him because of Houston Endowment. I had met Dalton at a luncheon in Galveston, in which awards were presented to the Seaborne Conservation Corps cadets, and afterward the endowment had made a $500,000 gift to the Conservation Corps, and after that the secretary invited me to visit him in Washington.

I went to see Dalton on Tuesday, April 28, 1998, at 10:45 a.m.

He had a big office in the Pentagon. You had to go through two outer offices to get to it. There were beige carpets on the floor, I remember, and polished brass ornaments and shiny coffee tables everywhere, and on the wall paintings of great ships and great naval battles. There was one Marine Corps picture on the wall, an oil painting of the flag raising on Mount Suribachi, Iwo Jima, in 1945. I couldn't help but stare at that painting as Dalton stood up from behind his great desk, and came around to shake my hand.

"I'm glad to see you, Mr. Nelson," he said. Dalton was tall, handsome, and had a powerful handshake.

"You know, Mr. Dalton," I said, "you really should have some more Marine Corps pictures on your walls."

It wasn't a good beginning. We stood there, still shaking hands, and I felt like a small boy who had just wet his pants at school, maybe not enough to cause real trouble.

"Sit down," said Mr. Dalton. He motioned to one of the large leather chairs by a coffee table. I sat and he sat down across from me.

"Tell me about the Marine Corps," he said. He smiled a little when he said it.

And then it all came out. I told him about Lee Roy and Colonel Fox and the playa lake in Lubbock and Frank Stoppiello.

Dalton smiled and listened, and when I was done I felt very foolish. I clenched my teeth a little, and waited for my reprimand.

But Dalton seemed reflective. He looked up and away from me, to the paintings on the walls. His gaze tracked slowly across several of them.

"I, myself, was in the submarines from 1964 to 1969," he said. "We patrolled in the South China Sea off Vietnam, in case China or Russia should have entered the war."

He seemed reflective. He had been thinking about this, too.

"I'm a little older than you, Mr. Nelson," he said, still looking at the paintings more than me.

"I've thought about it a lot since then, you know," he continued. "Especially since I got this job," and here he swept his hand about the room.

Something more was coming.

"In this job I think of the ones who chose what Lee Roy chose. I think of them often, the young men and women who are willing to put on the uniform, and are willing to go out there to the far edge of American power, across the seas, and into the jungles and the mountains where on the next ridgeline or across the next river are those who hate us.

"Give us Lee Roy's story," he said.

"I have to tell you," he paused and looked down. "I have to tell you there are some days when I have my doubts about what it all means. Find Lee Roy for all of my young people, Mr. Nelson," he said. "Find Lee Roy for every man and every woman that I have to send out there. Give us Lee Roy's story and then tell it to everyone," he said, "so we will never forget it."

And then he smiled again, now the smile of the secretary of the navy, no longer that of John H. Dalton, human. He stood, walked to the door, opened it, and asked a photographer to come in.

During the picture taking, Mr. Dalton beamed and I smiled. As we stood there, he said sideways to me, still facing the camera,

"Whatever I can do to help you with your work, I will do. You just let me know."

Photos were taken. I walked out of the secretary's office. I went down the elevator and walked out through the lobby doors. It was cool and sunny outside, and I was thinking out my plans to find Lee Roy.

I went back to Lubbock, for starters. Not right away, but after I had thought about things for a while. Texas Tech University has a bimonthly alumni magazine called the *Techsan*, and one of its writers, Jeff Whitley, had called me about an interview earlier in the year. Because of Houston Endowment, the *Techsan* wanted to profile me as a featured "successful alumnus." I wasn't comfortable with that kind of thing, and I hadn't agreed to do it right off, but now I could see a purpose in it. Instead of talking about myself, I thought I would do the interview back in the Administration Building at Texas Tech, and I would tell Lee Roy's story.

I drove from Houston to Lubbock in the fall of 1998, and I went alone. That's generally how I have done it when I have returned there, I can't say exactly why.

I stayed in the Holiday Inn alongside the highway that Lubbockites call the South Loop. I still have friends from my youth there, and I could stay with them, but this is how I have always done it. I stay at the Holiday Inn so I can draw the fabric curtains open at the end of the days and look out the windows across the fields to the west.

I parked in the visitors' lot on the Texas Tech main campus, close by the great bronze statue of Will Rogers sitting atop his horse. Then I walked up the stone steps to the Administration Building, to the Alumni Affairs offices on the second floor, and I waited for Jeff Whitley.

I liked Jeff right away when I met him. He was young, bright, and true; he was interested in people's stories; and he could listen. That's a powerful skill, the ability to really hear what someone is saying. We sat in his office that day, books lining one wall, magazine issues stacked up on tables, pictures of Texas Tech hanging everywhere on the walls, and we talked.

That is, I talked. I told Jeff about Lee Roy. I told him about our playa lake conversations, PLC camp, A Shau Valley, and law school. I talked about Martie and Danny and Frank Stoppiello. I'm not usually much of a talker, but I was that day. And Jeff Whitley listened.

When it was over, Jeff said he would write it the way I had told it. He would write of David Nelson telling the story of his friend Lee Roy Herron, a hero who had been killed in A Shau Valley in 1969 and so never been able to grow up and become the person he might have been.

I liked it. The alumni magazine for Texas Tech University interviewed me for my story, and I told them about Lee Roy.

When the *Techsan* article appeared in 1999, however, it wasn't as I had imaged it. It wasn't just about Lee Roy. It was about the two of us. It had us intertwined from the playa lake conversations up to the present. I had trouble with this at first. Every living Tech alumnus would be reading this article, and I was troubled that they would all be getting it mixed up, whether the article was about Lee Roy Herron or about David Nelson.

I didn't show it to Martie at first. I left it on my desk upstairs. I looked at it in the evening, when I changed my clothes after coming home from work. I tried to understand it.

After a while I showed it to Martie. She came into the study, sat on the sofa near the window, and read the article. I didn't say anything about it.

"It's about you and Lee Roy," she said.

"Yes," I said.

"I like it," she said.

I still didn't say anything.

"It shows you and Lee Roy kind of twined up together, still and before, almost like some of his spirit and some of his energy remains with you, inside you."

Martie laughed her soft laugh. "You don't think that's too weird, do you, David?"

You have to be careful what you say, even to your wife, because words can have their own way sometimes. You have to choose them just so.

"Well," I said, "Jeff Whitley must have seen it that way." It was careful, tactful, the way I put it to Martie. I liked it.

After Martie went back downstairs, I sat there in my study, looked out the window, and thought about it all.

I wasn't sure where I was headed with this now, as the millennium neared its end. But I had learned a lot from speaking with Jeff Whitley, so I resolved to find other people who had known Lee Roy, and to talk with them.

I called his mother, his sister, high school friends—Maureen Malley Peltier, Jimmy Davis, Bill Cox, Jr., Marcie Johnston Beasley, Cecil Puryear, Charles Lance. These people had been Lee Roy's friends, and they had been my friends, and Jeff Whitley had it right, because as I learned more about Lee Roy I learned more about myself.

All of these people, our circle, had grown up well—brave and strong and true. They hadn't necessarily become wealthy, but they were all involved in their communities, loyal to their families, respectful of the country and of God, just like me. I had come from them, these people of the southern plains, I was like them, and it had been good to grow up out there. I felt better about how it had all gone for me.

I drove to Lubbock to see Mrs. Herron. I felt nervous about it. I hadn't seen her since the sixties. Lee Roy's father had long since died of Alzheimer's disease, I had heard, and Jane—Jane must have grown up and might already have become a grandmother. It is a long drive from Houston to Lubbock, and as I drove I thought about all these things.

After a night in the Holiday Inn, I went to Mrs. Herron's house on 38th Street, just off University Avenue.

Lorea Herron had white hair now, and she seemed stooped and small. But her eyes were bright, and her mind was clear. She showed me a scrapbook she had kept about Lee Roy since he was a child. She had the book there on the table in front of us, as if he were still alive in it. In the front of the book was the photograph of the church service at Fire Support Base Razor.

Later that day, I drove over to see Jane Herron Graham, and she had the newspaper clippings from the *Avalanche-Journal* with the news of Lee Roy's death. She had some letters that Lee Roy had written home from Vietnam, and she gave me a folder full of them.

And then I went to Vietnam. I traveled with Texas Tech Chancellor John Montford; Jim Reckner, who was director of the Vietnam Center at Texas Tech; and Phil Price, president of the Vietnam Center advisory board. Together we crawled through Vietcong tunnels at Cu Chi. These are a tourist attraction now, with B-52 bomb craters and signs all about. We visited the Citadel in Hue—now rebuilt and a peaceful place. We went to Hanoi and visited the "Hanoi Hilton." We sat in a lecture room behind General Giap. We went to the Army Museum there and looked at the maps of roads and strategies from the North Vietnamese perspective.

In Vietnam I got the idea for a scholarship dedicated to the memory of Lee Roy. Talking with John Montford, Jim Reckner, and Phil Price, all of whom had served in Vietnam, and seeing the devastation that had been wrought upon that small country by both sides—I thought an education scholarship named after Lee Roy would be fitting. Lee Roy had believed strongly in education and had said several times that he would go back for an advanced degree once he was out of the Marine Corps.

I thought we would name it the Lee Roy Herron Memorial Endowed Scholarship, and that it would be administered through the Vietnam Center and Archive, which houses masses of documents from the Vietnam War but also supports educational programs and research into the causes and consequences of the war. It would be just right. Then, at least in that one place, Lee Roy would be forever, his story never forgotten.

There was one more thing. It was as John Dalton had said, and what I had known from the beginning: there would have to be this book.

[15]
March 3, 2001
The Ceremony

If we were going to have a Lee Roy Herron Scholarship, we would have to have a ceremony to launch it. I started to think seriously about that on the flight back from Vietnam. John Montford, Jim Reckner, Phil Price, and I had first discussed a ceremony while cruising along the Saigon River on an old Russian hydrofoil.

We would need a ceremony and some money to launch the scholarship. Because I'm both an accountant and a lawyer, I could think of several ways to do that.

Of course, we would have to get the approval of Texas Tech, but I figured that wouldn't be hard. On the flight back from Vietnam, Montford, the Texas Tech chancellor, agreed to the scholarship, as long as I raised the money.

We fixed a date for the ceremony: March 3, 2001. Texas Tech has a circular complex of buildings dedicated to international relations and education, situated just off Indiana Avenue, and Montford said we could use a reception room there. He said the room would be just right for what we were talking about, with the colors of many flags, and floor-length glass windows along the western wall. He was right. It wasn't the Hall of Mirrors at Versailles, but it was close enough.

A handful of Lubbock High friends and I began to raise money for the scholarship in the summer of 2000. Jeff Whitley and Jeff McLain, both at Texas Tech, volunteered to help. I started the process by writing to all the Lubbock High graduates from the class of 1963. I included a biographical brochure of Lee Roy, ably drafted by Jeff McLain. Pretty much everybody gave what they could. I was relieved. It became clear to me that we would have over $30,000 to give by ceremony day.

Early March in West Texas can be difficult. March 3, 2001, was windy and cold. The sun was out early, but that could change quickly.

It was late in the afternoon when people began arriving at the oval room in the center of the Hall of Nations at Texas Tech, with the flags of many nations all about the edges, and brightly lit display cases in the center. Lee Roy's dress blue uniform was there, folded as he must have left it thirty years before. The dark blue and stark white markings of the Navy Cross were upon it. His Mameluke sword was there, too, resting at the side of the uniform. People had brought and set out other things they remembered from Lee Roy's time with them—a high school yearbook, letters, black-and-white photos from long ago. Jeff McLain displayed a number of the items on a large bulletin board for the crowd to view.

Colonel Fox was there, not in uniform, but with his Medal of Honor around his neck.

A number of the guys from Alpha Company, I-9, were there. George Malone, the commander of 1st Platoon. Charles "Doc" Hudson, the corpsman. Other Alpha Company marines from across the country included Ted Decker, Oscar Borboa, Tony Romero, and Pete Giacchetta. Andy Vaart was there, too.

I didn't know whether Danny would come or not. Lee Roy's

Fellow Marines gathered at the March 3, 2001, ceremony to honor Lee Roy Herron display a bronze relief of Lee Roy crafted by his classmate Norman Flanagan. From left to right: George Malone, Tony Romero, Ted Decker, Wesley Fox, David Nelson, Charles "Doc" Hudson, Andy Vaart, Oscar Borboa, and Pete Giacchetta. Author's personal collection.

David Nelson as master of ceremonies presides at the March 3, 2001, ceremony to honor Lee Roy Herron and to present a scholarship bearing Lee Roy's name to the Vietnam Center at Texas Tech University. Seated guests on the near side front row include (right to left): Lorea Herron (dark jacket), Jane Herron Graham (white jacket), Bennie Davis (white outfit), and Lee Roy Herron's widow, Danelle (dark outfit). Author's personal collection.

widow hadn't responded to my invitations, and I didn't call her because I just didn't want to pressure her. But she came, along with her mother, Bennie. Her husband and her children did not come, and I could understand that. I hadn't seen Danny since before Lee Roy was killed. She seemed small and thin. Danny had always worn a cross on her neck in the old days, but that was gone. When she came in, under the lights in the reception area, I knew right away that it was Danny. I went up, took her hand, and told her how glad I was that she had come. She didn't say much. I would be the master of ceremonies that day, and I could tell that it wouldn't be right to ask her to speak.

Mrs. Herron came, walking in on the arm of her daughter, Jane Herron Graham. Lorea walked slowly, smiled at me, and came up at about the same time that Danny had come. I introduced the two—how strange that was, introducing Lee Roy's wife to his mother, as if they didn't know each other. They stood apart together and they spoke, and I do not know what was said.

I wasn't sure if Charles Lance would come that day. He had always been friendly when I had talked with him on the phone, but he had never said for sure that he would come. I think that for many of these people who had really known Lee Roy, the ceremony was a mixed thing. It was easier for those who hadn't really known Lee Roy, or who had known him more as an idea. For them, there were no painful memories about it. It was all beautiful and honorable.

James H. Davis did not come. Lieutenant Davis, commander of 2nd Platoon, had been hit by mortar fragments in the assembly area along the streambed on the day of Lee Roy's death, just as Lieutenant Fox was giving the attack order for 2nd Platoon, the order Lee Roy would have to carry out. I had written to Davis several times, but from his replies I could tell that there was something too painful about this and that he couldn't do it. He did tell me that, like Lieutenant Malone, he had made the Marine Corps a career, and that he had been involved in other fights, including the assault on Koh Tang, Cambodia, May 15, 1975, as part of the *Mayaguez* rescue. After retiring from the Marine Corps, Davis was now working for the CIA.

I did not know many who came to the ceremony that day. They were of all ages. Some brought children. I don't know if they were Texas Tech people, Lubbock community members, or what. I couldn't meet them all. But I can say that when it came time for us to move out of the reception area into the lecture room on the west side of the Hall of Nations, every seat was taken, and people had to stand in the back and along the walls on the sides.

It was time, 4:00 p.m. Some of the staff began to move people into the lecture room. I took one last look at Lee Roy's uniform, lying on the display case under the lights, then turned and walked to the front of the lecture room, where a lectern was situated with some seats in front of tall windows facing west.

A Marine Corps honor guard posted the colors from the rear of the room, marching to a drum cadence along the center aisle. Everyone stood. I placed my hand across my left breast. There was not a noise in the room, not even from the children.

I opened the ceremony by reading Lee Roy's Navy Cross citation, signed by John H. Chafee, secretary of the navy, over a year after the action, on February 24, 1970.

I had invited Colonel Fox to speak first, to describe the day of Lee Roy's death to those who hadn't been there, and to those too young to have memories of the Vietnam War. He described the jungle, gunfire, and casualties, and spoke of his own decision making that day. In the heat of the moment, under enemy fire, he

THE UNITED STATES OF AMERICA

THIS IS TO CERTIFY THAT
THE PRESIDENT OF THE UNITED STATES OF AMERICA
HAS AWARDED THE

NAVY CROSS

TO
FIRST LIEUTENANT LEE R. HERRON
UNITED STATES MARINE CORPS RESERVE

FOR
EXTRAORDINARY HEROISM
WHILE ENGAGED IN MILITARY OPERATIONS
ON 22 FEBRUARY 1969

GIVEN UNDER MY HAND IN THE CITY OF WASHINGTON
THIS 24TH DAY OF FEB 1970

SECRETARY OF THE NAVY

Lee Roy Herron was posthumously awarded the Navy Cross (second only to the Medal of Honor) for extraordinary heroism and valor in combat. Courtesy of the Herron family.

had known that Alpha Company would have to do something quickly to reduce the intensity of fire from the hillside above or face possibilities too bitter to contemplate. He ended by saying that although many of us at the ceremony were getting along in years, Lee Roy would be "remembered forever at Texas Tech as a hard-charging, young marine lieutenant."

I stood to the side as he spoke. When I glanced out the windows, I saw the blue-black curvy lines of a weather front coming across the plains.

Andy Vaart spoke next, because he had noticed Lee Roy in the *Navy Times* photograph of the church service in the shell crater on Fire Support Base Razor. We had an enlargement of the photo mounted on a tripod at the front of the room, that image of Lee Roy in prayer, and Vaart referenced it:

The President of the United States takes pride in presenting the NAVY CROSS posthumously to

FIRST LIEUTENANT LEE R. HERRON
UNITED STATES MARINE CORPS RESERVE

for service as set forth in the following

CITATION:

For extraordinary heroism while serving as Executive Officer, Company A, First Battalion, Ninth Marines, Third Marine Division in the Republic of Vietnam on 22 February 1969. While patrolling north of Ashau Valley in Quang Tri Province, the lead elements of Company A came under intense fire and were pinned down by a large North Vietnamese Army force. First Lieutenant Herron maneuvered one of his platoons forward to reinforce the lead elements. When the second platoon commander was seriously wounded, he immediately assumed command and quickly organized the men into an assault force. Skillfully deploying his men, he led them in an aggressive attack until halted and pinned down by an extremely heavy volume of cross-fire from several enemy machine guns augmented by mortar, rocket-propelled grenade, small arms, and automatic weapons fire from the North Vietnamese emplacements, as well as numerous sniper positions in trees in the dense jungle canopy. Undaunted by the hostile rounds impacting around him, First Lieutenant Herron repeatedly exposed himself to enemy fire as he moved among his men to encourage them and urged them to inch forward to positions from which they could deliver more effective return fire. Aware that the fire from two mutually supporting hostile machine guns was holding his Marines in place and preventing the removal of the casualties, he completely disregarded his own safety as he exposed himself to North Vietnamese fire to direct a light antitank assault round which scored a direct hit on one of the machine gun bunkers. Boldly leaping to his feet, he fearlessly charged across the fire-swept terrain to hurl hand grenades and fire his weapon against the enemy emplacement, killing nine North Vietnamese soliders who were in the bunker. While directing his men in the assault on the remaining bunker, First Lieutenant Herron was mortally wounded by enemy sniper fire. His heroic actions inspired his men to such aggressive action in coordinated company attack that 105 North Vietnamese soldiers were killed and the large bunker complex destroyed. By his courage, bold initiative and unwavering devotion to duty, First Lieutenant Herron upheld the highest traditions of the Marine Corps and the United States Naval Service. He gallantly gave his life for his country.

For the President,

John J.J. Chafee

Secretary of the Navy

Lee Roy Herron's Navy Cross citation describes his extraordinary heroism on February 22, 1969. Courtesy of the Herron family.

Warfare provides searing images. Men who go to combat have albums full in their minds. Many dramatic ones have been captured in print by great combat photographers. . . . These photographs often capture the violence, destruction, pain, and fear of combat. In my experience, never has a photograph captured the spirituality of men at war as well as this one. That Lee should last be photographed in that way speaks more about him than I could possibly offer. I hope by having noticed it, I brought added comfort to his family and friends.

It turned out that Vaart had worked with James Davis at the CIA. Although Davis did not attend the ceremony, he had entrusted Vaart with a personal letter, which Vaart read:

Lee Herron was one of those rare officers that knew how to truly accomplish the mission and take care of the welfare of the officers and troops within his command. In fact, Lee went beyond the call of duty in all that he did during the short time I was blessed with his companionship.

Lee joined Alpha Company as the Executive Officer prior to Operation Dewey Canyon. When he came around the company to introduce himself it was immediately apparent to all of us that he was sincere and concerned about not only his role in the Alpha Company family of Marines, but he wanted to share our concerns, our fears, and our hopes. It was not long before Lee and I became personal friends as we looked over the mountains surrounding the fire support base and shared our deepest thoughts and concerns. Men do this when they are far away from home and family in time of war, and Lee was good at comforting us as he learned more about us as individuals.

One story that really has stayed with me over the years typifies Lee as a person. When the Company had no chaplain in the field for several Sundays, Lee suggested that the two of us hold services for the troops, and encouraged me to write home for materials that my mother had because my father was a Methodist minister. I did so, and we did as Lee suggested, we held services for the troops.

When Alpha Company was ambushed on 22 February 1969 it was Lee who made the sacrifice and took over my platoon after I was wounded, and he died bravely leading my platoon forward into the intense enemy fire that was the norm that day. Lee was as brave as he was righteous, moral, and gentle. One thing I can say about Lee Herron, when I was around him, I was the man I wanted to be, not the man I knew I was. I will never forget Lee Herron. He has been in my thoughts every day since the day he gave his life for his country, his fellow Marines, and the mission, and I am a better person for his memory.

God Bless Him.

I knew that Lee Roy's mother would give her blessing to the ceremony. No one had a stronger relationship with Lee Roy—in life and in death; she had understood him both ways. I invited her to the podium.

Mrs. Herron stood up straight from her front-row seat and paused a moment. Then she walked to the podium, taking small steps, with her daughter, Jane, beside her. I had to lower the microphone so that she could speak into it.

Mrs. Herron spoke briefly and read a quote from Lee Roy's widow, Danny, something she'd said to a newspaper reporter shortly after Lee Roy's death:

Lee Roy Herron had played war all his life, waiting for the day when he could defend his country against aggressors as his patriotic heroes had done in the past on the pages of history books that were to have been his life work. He was so proud of America. Just imagine a big guy like that getting tears in his eyes when they played "The Star Spangled Banner." In the morning and especially at five in the afternoon, regardless of where we were [at the Defense Language Institute], we stopped to listen and be silent. He would have been so proud. It was on George Washington's birthday [that Lee Roy was killed]. He was so proud of his country. Most people don't feel that way nowadays.

Then Lt. Col. George Malone spoke. On the right of Alpha Company that day, Lieutenant Christman with 3rd Platoon had been grievously wounded and died before evacuation. In the center with 2nd Platoon, Lee Roy had been killed. Only on the left, with 1st Platoon, had a platoon commander been able to walk away from the hillside that day: George Malone.

Malone, too, had been awarded the Navy Cross for his actions that day, February 22, 1969. He had been wounded but he had survived. George had made the Marine Corps a career afterward, and become a lieutenant colonel.

"Where does a nation find men such as Lee Roy Herron?" Malone asked the audience. "Well, it found one in Lubbock, Texas, and we were proud to know and to serve with him."

Charles "Doc" Hudson, there in A Shau Valley that day, is a medical doctor in the Houston area now. He spoke, looking at Lorea Herron in the front row. "Mrs. Herron," he said. "Were it not for your son that day, we all would have perished. We are here to thank you, not only for Lee Roy, but for our lives as well."

A few of Lee Roy's close friends, Bill Cox, Jr., Jimmy Davis, and Charles Lance, spoke of instances that displayed Lee Roy's kindness and devotion to God, country, family, and friends. Jane Herron Graham told both humorous and serious tales of Lee Roy's childhood and of his deep sense of honor and duty.

Tony Romero was there. I didn't know who he was, but he introduced himself to me, a short, dark-haired Mexican American who had learned of the ceremony and came that day, driving from New Mexico. He remembered that Lee Roy had taken a personal interest in him when he had reported to 1/9 at Vandegrift. Lee Roy had asked him where he was from, and Romero sensed a kindness beneath Lee Roy's marine officer exterior. Romero, who had asked to be transferred from mail detail to Alpha Company so he could be with Lee Roy, survived the February 22 battle. After leaving the Corps later, he had returned home to New Mexico where he taught boxing to Latino kids.

Texas Tech University Chancellor John T. Montford was there in the Hall of Nations that day. Chancellor Montford had been a prominent attorney from West Texas, who had risen in Texas politics to become a senior member of the Texas Senate and head of the Senate Finance Committee. Some said that Chancellor Montford had to have a bodyguard named Bubba with him pretty much continuously after he had left the Senate and come back to Lubbock, where he was from. I can't say whether that was true. But I knew that John Montford had been in the Marine Corps in the sixties, a lawyer—JAG Corps—like me. I also knew that he had been in Vietnam a time or two, to try cases or do some investigations, though he said nothing of that at the ceremony for Lee Roy.

We had raised $33,000 for the scholarship in Lee Roy's name, and I presented a huge check to Chancellor Montford. I felt good about the Lee Roy Herron Memorial Endowed Scholarship, and smiled broadly when I turned to shake the chancellor's hand.

When I turned away, I caught a glimpse through a window of storm clouds coming closer.

The last thing we did at the ceremony that day was to unveil a work of art. I had asked our classmates at Lubbock High what we could give at the ceremony from our class, and it turned out that Norman Flanagan had become an artist, a sculptor. He worked in bronze, making likenesses of people, and he offered to make a bronze of Lee Roy if the rest of us agreed. We did. Flanagan had been working on it for many months, none of us had seen it, and it was covered with red silk in the front of the room at the ceremony.

Now Lorea Herron and Jane Herron Graham came up again to unveil it. Flanagan stood by. When Lee Roy's mother and sister pulled a cord, the red silk drifted down and the face of Lee Roy was there, dark in bronze, looking straight at us.

At that very moment, storm winds crashed against the full-length windows of the Hall of Nations. There was fury in it. Rains lashed the windows in angled sheets, and there was lightning. The lights were already low in the hall, but then it became very dark as the storm washed over us. No one spoke, and four of us stood there next to Lee Roy's statue. I don't believe in signs and omens, but this was not good.

The ceremony ended after that, and people walked out, but I don't remember this. I remember the storm. I remember standing there with Norman Flanagan and Lee Roy's mother and sister, with the red silk lying on the floor and rain lashing the windows. That's what I remember.

• • •

On May 17, 2002, Jennifer Board, a Texas Tech University graduate student in history, was awarded the first Lee Roy Herron scholarship. She went to Vietnam to spend the summer working on her master's thesis comparing U.S. prisoner of war experiences in Korea and in Vietnam.

Lee Roy Herron's bronze relief, crafted by fellow junior high and high school classmate Norman Flanagan. The relief was unveiled at the March 3, 2001, ceremony to honor Lee Roy. Author's personal collection.

Epilogue

It was about a month later that I went back to Lubbock again. I told Martie that it was to see my mother, who was failing with the years, and that was true. But there was something else. I wasn't completely sure what it was, so I just said I was going to visit my mother.

I drove alone from Houston, wanting to feel things in my life, and to think things through. You have to be alone for times like that.

It was a Friday in April 2001. I visited with my mother that evening. The next morning I drove over to Mrs. Herron's house, and we then went together to the cemetery. She brought a bouquet of flowers.

We parked in the Resthaven Cemetery parking lot, off Nineteenth Street, just inside the Loop. It marks the perimeter of the city proper, a concrete boundary of arches and whining engines from the long-distance trucks.

It was still early morning when we got there. I'm an early riser, and so was Mrs. Herron, and it was a good time because nobody else was there.

We stepped out of the car, and I looked out across the great green expanse of trees and lawns, damp and twinkling in the early sun. I had seen it before, many times, but I looked at it differently that day. It was a good place. Lee Roy lay there somewhere, and it was a good day in the Southwest. I understood then that I had come to say goodbye. This may sound silly, but I think that in the back of my mind I had secretly assumed that Lee Roy would just come back some day—just show up on the porch of some house where I was, and say that he'd had a hard time, but now he was back and he would tell me the stories of it all. Or something like that.

Mrs. Herron knew the way: a short distance north, along rows of bronze plate markers in the earth, in the center of a great lawn.

We walked slowly, but I didn't mind. It was quiet as we walked, and we felt the dew in the grass and the sun coming up across our backs.

We passed close by my father's grave. I pointed to the place for Mrs. Herron, where he was, Edmund Nelson. There was an open space next to him for my mother. We crossed two rows of bronze markers to that place, and we stood by it.

"I knew him, you know," she said. "At the Estacado school, in the third grade," she said. She took one flower from the bouquet in her hand, one of the red ones, I think, and she placed it down along the edge of where my father lay.

"I couldn't stay in the school too long," she said. "We were poor, and I couldn't stay." She didn't say it to complain. She was just saying how it had been at that time, standing there with me by my father's place.

It was only fifty feet farther to the place where Lee Roy lay. There was a live oak there, and we stood by the tree looking down at Lee Roy's marker. Mrs. Herron laid the flowers across the marker, so they touched the metal frame and made a gar-landed edge to it. The sun in our faces, I thought of Lee Roy, how he might look down there, if we could see him. And I thought of Lee Roy as a little boy, Lee Roy as a college student, and Lee Roy the way he looked back at me that day in the dormitory when he asked if I was coming or not when it was time to go to the PLC camp.

It seemed to me that there should be solemnity and silence at this moment, but it wasn't that way. I started to talk.

"I remember how it was when we were little boys," I said. "I remember how we played at recess. I remember how he talked when we were in junior high school and how he threw his tennis racquet in the lake that day. He was so mad," I said. "I remember when we went to Texas Tech, how he was so patriotic, so mad at the hippies." I paused. "Not that we had any hippies at Texas Tech," I said. And then I laughed. It didn't seem right, but I started to laugh and I couldn't stop for a while.

"But do you know," I said, talking to Mrs. Herron but looking down at where Lee Roy's remains lay. "Do you know, sometimes I can't remember him as a marine, with the uniform and all, you know?" I looked at her. This was embarrassing for me. "I can't remember him as a marine sometimes," I said. And then I think I was starting to cry, so I looked away.

We stood there silently together.

"Sometimes I can't remember that, either," she said.

Lee Roy Herron's grave marker at Resthaven Cemetery, Lubbock, Texas. Author's personal collection.